Unbroken Vows

Unbroken Vows

KEEPING IT TOGETHER

DENNIS S. NICKENS

AKA "THE SPIRITUAL ROMEO"

Published by Spines
ISBN: 979-8-89569-038-3

This book is dedicated to my parents, Dennis and Amelia Nickens. You are amazing, and I thank God for you.

Contents

Preface

From my perspective and understanding of what the Word of God teaches, I believe that God is victorious in everything that He does. Subsequently, I believe that if you build your marriage on the Word of God and put all your faith and trust in His words, you will enter into a marriage the way God designed you to; and when you do, the only outcome you will spiritually see is victory.

The enemy is motivated to place stumbling blocks in your path, but in Christ, you possess the power to re- move those stumbling blocks and to make your pathway for your marriage smooth. Be like a track star and run your race, anticipating ahead of time how to attack the straightway as well as the curves.

May this book help you pace yourself as you move forward to victory in your relationship.

Dennis Nickens

CHAPTER 1

Marriage Is...

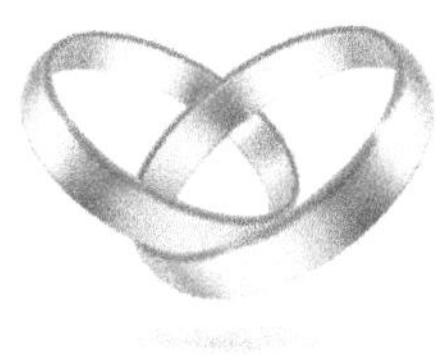

A man shall ... hold fast to his wife.
– Genesis 2:24 (ESV)

MARRIAGE, noun

The act of uniting a man and woman for life; wedlock; the legal union of a man and woman for life. Marriage is a contract, both civil and religious, by which the parties engage to live together in mutual affection and fidelity till death shall separate them.

Marriage was instituted by God himself for the purpose of

- preventing the promiscuous intercourse of the sexes, for

- promoting domestic felicity, and for

- securing the maintenance and education of children.

– Webster's Dictionary 1828[1]

GOD'S IDEA

Marriage is for those who trust and believe in construct- ing a union based on what the Bible teaches:

1. *God is at the center of the marriage–* At the beginning of the Bible, you can find our heavenly Father (God) establishing the foundation of a marriage. He put it together with Himself at its center. It was never in the plan for two people to build a relation- ship without Him being its focus.
2. *God established the foundation of the family–* Marriage provides a solid foundation in which to raise children.
3. *God has designed us for intimacy–* Through Adam and Eve, God authorized a man and a woman to come together as one, which completes the holy union and keeps them closely connected to each other.
4. *Marriage reflects that we are His covenant people–* God approved of a man and a woman to be together for life. "Therefore a man shall leave his father and his mother and hold fast to his wife, and they shall become one flesh" (Genesis 2:24 ESV). This is a mirror of God's covenant relationship with us, both during and after life on earth.

Being married is a beautiful thing. It is the heart of the Father.

He is committed to protecting your marriage. He does not provide anyone with the authorization to destroy those He brings together.

GOD'S MARRIAGE MODEL

Technology companies Apple, Microsoft, Sony, and Hewlett-Packard have developed formulas that have turned their businesses into successful corporations that others model their businesses after. Within the success of these companies, there is one thing all have in common: they established a foundation with strong pillars (vision) to hold up the success of these fruitful companies. If you ever have an opportunity to visit one of these companies' sites, you will be able to see their company vision posted everywhere. The leadership displays the vision throughout each location for the purpose of ensuring that every employee captures the vision and runs with it. Everyone being linked to a single vision helps to prevent a different vision from coming in and causing division within the company. The same idea is critical for having a successful marriage. "Where there is no revelation, people cast off restraint; but blessed is the one who heeds wisdom's instruction" (Proverbs 29:18). The correct application of God's foundation for marriage causes people to stick and stay, while the misuse of this foundation causes them to run and leave.

Know that God has a good model for your marriage, and He plants Himself at the heart of why you are together. Having confidence in Him and His ways reduces the pressure of feeling like you have to do everything.

When you let Him train you up for the purpose of being an indissoluble force, you are automatically part of His winning strategy for your marriage. His training will develop you and push you past what you are willing to do, but you need to be that spouse who is willing to get things done to make your marriage great. Patience builds up a go-getter mentality. Be living proof that you possess the vision and aptitude to dream big.

The Father's presence in your marriage gives you the faith to believe that, despite what you may face, the blueprint of a godly marriage places its arms around the Word of God, and His truth will not allow anything to convince you to let go. God knows all and does all things through a process. God leaves us marriage seeds everywhere, and each one contains all the nutrients needed for the marriage to be productive. If you apply what the Word of God says to your marriage, it will overflow with blessings that are beneficial to others. In having the Word as the authority for your marriage, you have an expectation—faith—of what God (and not man) is able to accomplish on your behalf.

It is a beautiful thing to recognize that hearing God is the way to know the true direction of which way your marriage should go. I advise you to learn how to conform your ear to be able to clearly hear what He is communicating to you. Conforming your earmeans that you possess the desire to hear the truth about what He sees in your relationship for the purpose of making it better, which allows you to live in a marriage that's full of life. He gives you access to this life. He provides you an opportunity to open a door that was designed to be opened. Ask yourself if you possess the key that unlocks the door to a marriage that's being fulfilled

—the door to life. "Jesus said to him, 'I am the way and the truth, and the life. No one comes to the Father except through me'" the key that opens the door to fulfillment is Jesus. Only through Him can we travel to a fulfilling marriage, one that makes us and our heavenly Father well pleased.

GOD'S WAYS ARE PERFECT

God has given us indestructible pillars that hold the weight of the marriage. Each one of these pillars carries the weight equally but is applied to the marriage separately. Family, I need you to see and use these pillars. Capture a good understanding as to why God created your marriage and made it indestructible. The spirit of the godly marriage starts with the foundation, which is His love; then it moves to the pillars:

1. Oneness - with God and each other
2. Obedience - to God, commitment to each other
3. Holiness - and trusting each other
4. Communication - with God and each other
5. Respect - honor, kindness, forgiveness
6. Faith - vision
7. Investments - in your marriage

In addition to His presence, the Word of God gives us these pillars to complete the marriage. Your marriage does not operate under the laws of the world but under His grace given to us freely ("Against such things there is no law" Galatians 5:23). Family, your marriage is not under a law designed to prevent your marriage from ex- celling; it is under grace. There are no limits on the potential inside you, and the grace of God sets your mar- riage up to grow.

It's God's love that is everything, not ours. Don't operate in rules of behavior that confine a marriage. God has established the structure for a godly marriage—His foundation of love—and as soon as you understand what your marriage is established on, you are prepared to be the spouse you believe the Father desires you to be.

WHAT MARRIAGE IS NOT

First, I must remove a philosophy that comes from the pit of hell. It comes against the foundation of what God has established as a marriage. Some people have been deceived by the enemy to get them to believe that what God has determined as the truth is not true. The goal of the enemy is to have people build their marriages from a foundation designed to destroy marriage. The philosophy I am speaking of has people believing that two people of the same sex can come together in a holy union. Based on what has been communicated in the Word of God, this is something that has never been ordained by God.

To establish understanding, I introduce two points to help you understand why this should not be a foundation for your marriage:

Love- I have heard people who desire to be with someone of the same sex use love as their justification. I have sought God's face and studied the Bible. In trusting the holy Word of God as the foundation for everything, I can find no reference from Him that would justify two people of the same sex being together in holy matrimony.

On the contrary, the Bible forbids people of the same sex to be together. "If a man lies [intimately] with a male as if he were a woman, both men have committed a detestable (perverse, unnatural) act; they shall most certainly be put to death; their blood is on them" (Leviticus 20:13 AMP). This Scripture tells us it is inappropriate for a person to engage in a relationship that does not have the ability to receive what the body was designed to receive. You can see that this act is something God does not approve because He called it "detestable"—which lets you know this type of act infuriates God. The Father hates it so much. Even if the student is trying to tell the teacher that what God is teaching is incorrect, I am here to let you know that God, as our perfect teacher, knows what He is doing. He is never wrong, nor is the instruction He has passed down to us.

Sex- People of the same sex engaging in a relationship was never justified or naturally authorized by God. If not, how would we be able to reproduce and replenish the earth? Naturally, the body makes it clear our bodies were not created to engage in an intimate relationship with a person of the same sex. Those who do are engaging in something that will bring an end to mankind. Based on what I have read and understand, there is only one right way of engaging in an authorized relationship—the way that will allow you to reproduce and replenish this earth. If you are not out to replenish the earth, that means you are out to destroy it.

It was established by our heavenly Father and is communicated throughout the Bible: a marriage is between a man and a woman. If that is not settled in your heart, it will be almost impossible for your marriage to last because building a marriage can only be done right on God's solid, indestructible foundation.

YOUR COMMITMENT

The foundation of all marriages is built on this thing called love —but whose love? If you have a conversation with someone who is about to get married, and you ask them why they want to be married to their future spouse, the first thing they usually say is that it's because they love them. Family, I am here to let you know that love should never be the only reason you are getting married to a person. Marriage takes so much more.

Your vows hold you accountable to doing marriage God's way. I pray that those vows push you and your spouse into greatness. Being married means that I must show myself responsible by being committed to what the Word of God says pertaining to a marriage—with all the love, faithfulness, humility, selflessness, and honesty He gives. Your marriage is designed to hold you accountable to love.

No one said your marriage is not going to face some rocky seas, but the GSP (God's spiritual perspective) that directs your marriage is equipped to provide you with information on how to deal with each storm when it comes. When your relationship with God is a priority, your relationship with your spouse can produce good results. It is possible to leave a marital legacy behind that will make your heavenly Father proud and others willing to follow.

Your marriage is supposed to be like taking in a majestic view—where you enjoy the moments and appreciate the things that surround you. "Rejoice! Be made complete [be what you should be], be comforted, be like-minded, live in peace; [enjoy the spiritual well-being experienced by believers who walk closely with God]; and the God of love and peace [the source of lovingkindness] will be with you" (2 Corinthians 13:11 AMP). Rejoice before God based on your success in not giving up and getting past the places that caused you to have doubts about what you are able to accomplish.

As you keep walking in this amazing marriage, desire to work on it with your spouse. God is aiming you at the target of a strong relationship with each other. God, who is the master of everything, will give you both more than enough confidence if your hearts are open to be fed with the appropriate amount of knowledge and understanding about how you should conduct yourselves in your marriage. Coming together in oneness and being able to dwell together in harmony is the key. Learn how to work things out. You'll be shown areas in your life you need to improve in together, and God will continue to work with you both to ensure that you get it right. Being able to get things to flow in the appropriate direction requires a willingness to work together. When you can move as a unified unit, all things work together to help the marriage excel.

Your perspective of your marriage can be like a precious gift. The only way to be able to view the gift is to first open the wrapper. To understand the gift, you must be willing to put in the time with it. To be able to appreciate the gift, you have to come to a place of agreement of accepting what it is. It's not what your idea of perfection is. It's the gift you were given.

Everyone who has ever said "I do" before God desires to be in a marriage that's peaceful, even though people who do not respect the holy union of marriage think it is impossible. It's possible with God. You can be so tuned into God with your marriage that you can only see and hear positive things about it, which causes it to produce good fruit. God commands you to be strong and courageous and to stand up for what you believe in—His Word. Do not have any concerns or fears about how your marriage will produce good fruit; just know that it will come forth looking like pure gold because you know who is with you and how it was put together.

YOUR DESTINY, YOUR VISION

Having a fantastic marriage is in your hands. It's part of your destiny. Know that the great expectations you have for your marriage are obtainable. If you do not quit, your marriage will continue to move forward, eventually getting to the point when you will have passed thirty, forty, or even sixty-plus years together.

The goal for your marriage is to come to a place where the words that come out of your mouth reflect what the Word of God confirms in your heart. Your marriage will be a gift that dwells on His foundation. Build the vision for this within your heart, and your marriage will be like a magnetic force that attracts what it needs to build your relationship. Desire to be in a marriage that's growing and productive. A heart that's out to build fruit is pleasing in the sight of God. Stay true to your vision for marriage. Don't lower your expectations, which are built on God's promises. Together, you and God can do the things required that will give your marriage life.

It does not matter where you find yourself now. This book is designed to invite you to a place that will motivate you to be all that you can be in your marriage. The moment you commit to going to this place, you will realize that your time for building a great marriage is limited on this earth, and you will pick up the pace to go all in to get a marriage that meets your expectations. I pray you understand that you do not have time to waste on doing things that are not equipped to take your relationship to the next level. You need, and God desires for you to see, the mission of your marriage. Be responsible for your marriage "ship," which is designed and created for you. Come on board as a passenger with the expectation of enjoying the ride and reaching your destiny.

Know that God has spoken over your marriage and plants Himself at the heart of why you are together.

Having confidence in Him reduces the pressure of feeling like you have to do everything. There is a winning strategy in your ability to be trained up for the purpose of being an indissoluble force. This force will develop you and push you past what you are willing to do. You want to be that spouse who's willing to get things done. Patience builds up in you a go-getter mentality. Be living proof that you possess the aptitude to dream big.

GOD'S GRACE FOR MARRIAGE

To get the most out of a marriage, learn to get to a place where you dwell in God's grace—flexibility in doing things which express your heart's desire when they are connected to the will of the Father. That's what blesses a marriage. When you are in a marriage given to you by God, you know you have been given excellent guidelines with control and authority over the outcome.

The God we serve is not a spiritual Father who gives you something without attaching the right resources to it. The reason why people have so many issues in their marriages is because they have come to a place where they stop believing that the resources are available. The resources are attached to God's grace, and using His grace in your marriage has control over the outcome of it. The work of the Holy Spirit in the marriage exposes itself more and more as you move closer and closer to trusting what God's put in it.

Having an appreciation for a beautiful marriage should cause you to become humble, sit back, and enjoy the journey. Time does not stop for anyone. Before you blink your eyes, you'll both be in your eighties and celebrating your fiftieth or sixtieth wedding anniversary. When you've been with your spouse for this length of time, you are willing to do anything with and for them. The only way you've been able to stick to and stay in the relationship is because you've both received the hand and grace of God to relate in a healthy way. I encourage you to get familiar with the fact that you are going to need this thing called grace to be able to provide the right kind of service to your king or queen.

The beautiful thing about building your marriage under the umbrella of grace is that grace is made readily available to everyone who is willing to receive it. Marriage is a reflection of the One who created it. It is not something that's forced upon you but is something that's presented to you and received from a place of love. Operating your marriage by grace is a gift from God.

The day you said I do is the day our heavenly Father created the covenant on the relationship of the marriage. The seal over your marriage is powerful enough to allow you to be able to go through anything and possess everything that's needed for the marriage. The seal is what we use to protect us from the enemy to prevent him from coming in our life and causing tragic events from taking place. Just like the heavenly Father anointed Je- sus, when we received Him as our Lord and Savior, we, too, are anointed to change anything and everything in our marriage for the better.

TRYING TO END THE MARRIAGE

Having self-control builds up patience and eliminates excuses crafted to end a marriage. Excuses are some- thing that our heavenly Father cannot stand and will not tolerate. Your marriage was not created in a way where you go about doing whatever you want, making excuses as to why you cannot find joy in it.

You have been invited to enter into this thing called a marriage. Don't be like the guests invited to the wed- ding feast:

He said to him, "A man was giving a big dinner, and he invited many; and at the dinner hour he sent his slave to say to those who had been invited, 'Come; for everything is ready now.' But they all alike be- gan to make excuses. ... And the slave came back and reported this to his master. Then the head of the household became angry and said to his slave, ... 'I tell you, none of those men who were invited shall taste of my dinner.'"

— – LUKE 14:16–18, 21, 24 (NASB)

The man sent out a servant three times for the purpose of inviting people to this beautiful event. He had prepared for a certain number of people, but most of the guests made excuses so they wouldn't have to come. This situation is a clear depiction of people who are strug- gling to trust God in their marriage and of what God faces on a consistent basis.

The beautiful thing about God is that the type of relationship you have with Him is like the one you should have with your spouse. Once you enter into your marriage, what you speak out of your mouth doesn't count; it is about what you speak from the heart. The reason why people struggle in their marriages is that they neglect to put their whole heart into it. Seeing a spouse do this will have you wondering if the original invite came from a reliable source. When you do accept the invitation to marriage in the correct way and you enter in, a table is prepared for you like no other, just as Jesus said.

The marriage prepared for you by God has been constructed so that excuses are not allowed to enter in. Excuses reject the idea that a good marriage is something you can have. Trust and believe that your marriage has been designed so it can only function from the position of victory. The Holy Spirit residing at the center of your marriage creates a balance that stabilizes your marriage. Any issue you may face is an issue that can be dealt with because it only has a temporary residence, and you operate from a position that's successful. It is up to you how long these issues stay in your marriage. Never be afraid to address an issue at the deepest level so that it doesn't transform into a problem. A problem is a permanent structure that requires more effort and energy in order to remove it. Sadly, many people think divorce is the way to remove it. No, this just delays God's work in you.

Removing problems is possible by following blocks of instruction that have been tailored for the relationship— the foundation of the Word, the love of God, and the pillars of marriage given in the Word. These form a pathway for your marriage. When Moses allowed what he experienced in his past to affect how he saw his future, he made a lot of excuses as to why he was not the one who was called. His lack of trusting that God knew what He was doing caused God's anger to be directed at him (see Exodus 4). This is something you do not want to do.

Family, you do not want God's anger to be directed at you because you disrespected a relationship He put together. *Your marriage is ready to be taken to the next level.* In making excuses, we are communicating that we do not trust the building process. I encourage you to make the choice today that you are not going to make any more excuses pertaining to the enjoyment of your marriage. Be responsible.

Know that if you are not enjoying your marriage, it is a reflection of your unrealistic expectations. When expectations aren't met, it can make you feel like you are not being protected from the cares of this world, but these are just feelings. You can't build a marriage foundation on a feeling. Your feelings are like the wind that blows—it is strong enough to let you know it exists, but it lacks the power to hold you up for an extended period of time. Instead, place your hope in something that has a consistent history of building and supporting your marriage.

The Word of God is not just a foundation for your relationship, it is a guide that develops your marriage over time. You have been given a free will to make decisions based on your hope in His Word. This type of hope is not built on something tangible but on the foundation that holds your marriage to a standard. If the foundation of it is built on what the Word of God says, you will not look for excuses on why you are not able to meet certain expectations. You will be inspired, knowing you have been given power to make your marriage a holy example that's acceptable to the heavenly Father.

Remove any excuses that prevent you from showing others that having a healthy marriage is possible. Be someone who takes their vows seriously, and be deter- mined to live a joy-filled marriage. Ensure that the un- ion between you and God is your priority and the rela- tionship you have with your spouse is secondary. Con- tinue to be willing to develop in your marriage. Your de- velopment is a gift to the world.

Determine that your marital vows were recorded in heaven. Your marriage was designed to be a lifelong covenant. This eliminates all excuses you can think of for why you shouldn't be in this marriage. Be motivated to be an example of what making it to the end looks like.

The determination that divorce cannot and will not happen has to be in you. The Word of God is in your marriage for the main purpose of you both being one. Allow His light to shine through you. When it does, it will draw others. They'll inquire how to replicate what your marriage has done. Knowing that you are doing it right will energize your marriage. It will activate you to run for a lifetime, which is sustainable because your heart has expectations of God and not your spouse. In having your expectations in the right place, your efforts will cause your marriage to produce the right kind of fruit.

Like one of their famous slogans says, Ford cars are "Built to Last." Understand that your marriage is composed of the right stuff and built to last. You are pre- pared for what may come in your marriage. You can find a way to deal with situations that come up. Your experience of working through past experiences will ease your mind in knowing that you are going to emerge from the present situation victoriously.

VALUE YOUR MARRIAGE

God has given us such an excellent model to follow, just as He did with His directions to Moses for building the temple. Your marriage is like part of God's spiritual body—a temple that's designed and created for the Holy Spirit to dwell in. Your temple is valuable to God, and if it is valuable to Him, it should be precious to you. God is everything and everywhere, and He desires to have a relationship with everyone. Understanding the value of oneness and the relational blessings marriage brings, God sent the One He loves most on a mission to provide it. God has designed marriage as two becoming one because God hungers for our marriages to be profitable.

> Having been knit together in love, and attaining to all the wealth that comes from the full assurance of understanding, resulting in a true knowledge of God's mystery, that is, Christ Himself, in whom are hidden all the treasures of wisdom and knowledge.
>
> — – COLOSSIANS 2:2–3 (NASB)

Marriage that is profitable is created through the vision that appears from within. When you see it in your mind, you will be able to hold it in your hand. This is only possible if you trust and believe what was made, and you can do this by trusting that God makes good things. When you have the heart of the Father, you'll understand how valuable you are and how priceless your marriage is.

Your life on this earth is only for a short period. Every second is precious, and you should make sure that every second counts. If you understand this, you understand that you cannot waste your time doing something that's not beneficial to your life. You must take advantage of what is designed to be a blessing. Investing in your marriage to reflect the kingdom is not a waste of time.

Marriage is something to be treasured. "Marriage is to be held in honor among all [that is, regarded as something of great value]" (Hebrews 13:4 AMP). Every marriage that's built properly places the building focus on the foundation, not the face value of the marriage. Don't invest your energy in building a look. Your desire should be to invest your energy into what is going to be profitable—God's standards.

Love Is...

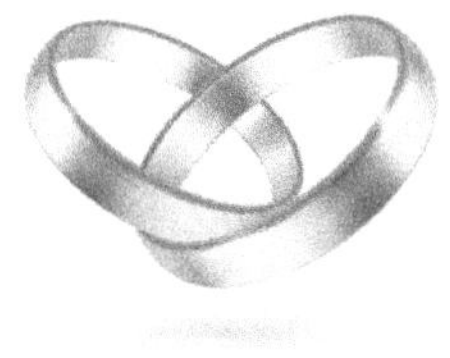

There is no fear in love.
– 1 John 4:18

LOVE, verb

[The sense is probably to be prompt, free, willing, from leaning, advancing, or drawing forward.]

1. In a general sense, to be pleased with; to regard with affection, on account of some qualities which excite pleasing sensations or desire of gratification.

LOVE, noun

1. An affection of the mind excited by beauty and worth of any kind or by the qualities of an object which communicate pleasure, sensual or intellectual. It is opposed to hatred. Love between the sexes is a compound affection, consisting of esteem, benevolence, and animal desire...

2. Courtship, chiefly in the phrase, to make love, that is, to court; to woo; to solicit union in marriage.

– Webster's Dictionary 1828[1]

GOD'S LOVE

The only way we can understand the true meaning behind the word "love" is by believing what that Scripture states: God is love. "Whoever does not love does not know God, because God is love" (1 John 4:8).

The Father gave His only begotten Son so you could know the love He has for you. This goes to show you how committed He is to having an unbreakable relationship with you. He was willing to give His Son in order for you to have access to something beautiful (*true* love) and in order to redeem the world, granting every man and woman access to His heart. Receiving His sacrifice is the only way to gain access to Him, and receiving His love is the only way He can deal with your heart to teach you the true meaning of love. God's love is what's needed as a foundation that will keep you in the marriage relationship and give you a faith-filled expectation of what God can do.

God created us on purpose. We're not on this earth just to be here. He created us out of His personal purpose for us. Your life is more valuable to God than it is to you, and He proved it more than two thousand years ago. "God demonstrates his own love for us in this: While we were still sinners, Christ died for us"

(Romans 5:8). God had you on His mind and knew what was needed, and He knew He had to send the Son to earth to give mankind access to His love.

Through love, He sent Jesus to pay the ultimate sacrifice. God the Father so loved us that He was willing to do what needed to be done to give us access to the kingdom of love. Getting access to the kingdom of love is not about a building or place but an unbreakable relationship with Him.

The love God has for you is bigger than any situation you potentially will face. He has placed His protection around you to protect you from things out to get you off course. For this reason, you should continue to develop your relationship with Him to be able to move forward in love. When you are in love with God, He will show you the true power that's within His love.

There is power and clarity in making yourself aware of the true meaning behind the word "beloved." The first part of this word, "be," is specific. It's a firm declaration to stay or live. "Loved" makes you think of a person intentionally treating you in a special way. When you bring the two words together, you see the type of relationship God the Father yearns to have with you.

Beloved, let us [unselfishly] love and seek the best for one another, for love is from God, and everyone who loves [others] is born of God and knows God [through personal experience]. The one who does not love has not become acquainted with God [does not and never did know Him], for God is love. [He is the originator of love, and it is an enduring attribute of His nature.]

— – 1 JOHN 4: 7–8 (AMP)

This is a very powerful Scripture that shows us where love comes from and how our love demonstrates who we know. When we know God, we know His love. The Scripture calls you out by calling you "beloved." Then, it continues with a call to unselfish love—love like His. His love in creating us and sacrificing His Son for us opens us up to letting Him do whatever He wishes in our lives.

> By this the love of God was displayed in us, in that God has sent His [One and] only begotten Son [the One who is truly unique, the only One of His kind] into the world so that we might live through Him. In this is love, not that we loved God, but that He loved us and sent His Son to be the propitiation [that is, the atoning sacrifice, and the satisfying of- fering] for our sins [fulfilling God's requirement for justice against sin and placating His wrath]. Beloved, if God so loved us [in this incredible way], we also ought to love one another.

— – VV. 9–11 (AMP)

This part of the Scripture should remove any barriers stopping you from believing you are not a priority in His eyes. The Father is a big enough God to be able to see everyone, and He can focus enough to develop a relationship with you independently. When John said, "Let us," he meant every unique individual plus

God, as one. You and God get to focus on loving others—the love you share with Him and have for Him brings out the best in you.

The best thing you can do in a relationship is identify the heavenly love that has been given to you that makes you someone who can transform the world. There should be nothing that stops you from falling in love with who you are in God.

GOD'S LOVE IS THE FOUNDATION YOUR MARRIAGE NEEDS

You can't afford to build your marriage on anything but God's love. Do not allow the godless thoughts of others to tell you how to conduct yourself in your marriage. If you allow this to happen, you become a puppet to them, and you allow them to control your life instead of God's love. I encourage you to cut the strings and become free. When you are free, you welcome the idea of being beloved.

Discern what is true, and know the plan of the enemy. He uses mankind itself to push people away from a loving relationship with God and causes them to believe that they can have a relationship that does not include Him.

God understands what it's going to take to get you to a place in Him where you can let go and let Him do what's needed for your relationship. He wants you to get to this place of understanding so you can feel His love.

The Father is willing to come get you from any situation that has you confined and in a place of turmoil and bring you into His love—a place of freedom and peace.

GOD LOVES MARRIAGE

God is such a loving Father. The love we have for Him is considered so small compared to His greater kind of love. Your marriage will manifest in a beautiful way when you understand the size of what's in you. The Son dwells inside you so you can show the world how to live for God and love others.

Being in love with God builds you up with a better understanding of what this love affair called marriage is all about. The fulfillment of love in God helps you believe that you can love a person for life because you have a better understanding of God's supply of everything you need to do so.

Jesus said, "A new command I give you: Love one another. As I have loved you, so you must love one another. By this, everyone will know that you are my disciples if you love one another" (John 13:34–35). In the new covenant, there is nothing He asks of us that He doesn't give us the power to do. I encourage you to keep in mind that because of your own one-of-a-kind, one-on-one relationship with God, you have the power to love well, too. If you're afraid of failure, think about the fact that everything you find yourself doing regularly had a first time, and even if that didn't work well, you had faith it would get easier. It is possible to love well not based on the results, but on the process, and over time, God gives you love to share with your spouse in your own unique way.

God the Father created you to be content and satisfied with the relationship that you have with Him but motivated to go after the call He has placed on you. You are a student of this thing called a marriage, and as a student, you must be willing to be taught how to be all that the Father has created you to be. Through love, He teaches you how to love yourself first before you transition in loving someone else. The best is yet to come. Continue to go through the process, knowing that He is not done with you yet. He will never stop helping, teach- ing, and supporting you. "The Advocate, the Holy Spirit, whom the Father will send in my name, will teach you all things and will remind you of everything I have said to you" (John 14:26). Identify with the idea that the Father's original intent was to create you as a lifelong student with a desire to continue being developed. When you truly know His love, you will experience His love for marriage too.

LOVE GOD FIRST

Family, I am here to help you understand that marriage is about doing things in the way that God created them to be done. That's the way I see it and the way God established it. It is impossible to fall out of love with your spouse when you have received the blessing upon the marriage that comes from God. That's why I say you need to make sure that you are in love with God before you even think about marriage and that you are not lusting after only the physical component of being in a relationship. Only one kind of love builds a relationship, and that is the relationship maintained in the presence of the One who established it. Staying in His presence shows Him that you are willing to be taught how to love the right way in order to have an effective relationship with your spouse.

The only way to really get to know God is to be in love with Him. If you are not in love with Him, it is impossible for you to be in love with your spouse. Being in love with God is what's needed to be able to build a foundation for your marriage. When you are connected and committed to God, it will keep you connected and committed to your spouse.

The Father makes it easy to receive what He's giving, but He so loves us that He is not going to force us to have a relationship with Him. Nothing hurts a parent more than desiring to have a relationship with their child while the child rejects that love. Even if your child rejects your love, you, as their parent, still have a desire to see them released from whatever has a hold of them, and you allow them to come back to you, no matter how hurt you feel. The only way this is possible is if they

1. come to their senses,
2. recognize what is real (which comes from God) and what is artificial (which comes from man), and
3. come back to the place of love.

When this happens, you are their biggest fan in celebrating the change with them. It's the same when God's love flows through you in a marriage. Your love causes you to wish only the best for your spouse and to always love first.

LOVE YOUR SPOUSE WITH GOD'S LOVE

"Love" is a versatile and powerful word that's used by people for the purpose of soothing themselves internally. I have found that the mistake most people make when it comes to their marriage is that they believe that earthly love is a strong enough substance to hold their marriage together. This is not the correct way of applying love to your marriage.

We should seek a deeper love with and for God and believe what the Word says pertaining to God being love. "Neither height nor depth nor anything else in all creation, will be able to separate us from the love of God that is in Christ Jesus our Lord" (Romans 8:39). It's puzzling to me to hear people talk about taking their relationship to the next level based on them being in love. They get married, time goes by, and you find these individuals in a place where the relationship has been destroyed because they've decided they are not in love anymore. The question I have for any couple who finds themselves in a situation like this is, *If you were in love with one another and it was blessed by God, how is it possible to be able to fall out of love with each other?*

It is important that you have a clear understanding of what God the Father is telling you every day. When He talks with you, He communicates as a leader, commanding you to do what He needs you to in your marriage. When you do these things, you will draw closer and develop a deeper understanding of what real love is all about. Trust and believe that God's goal is to have His people learn how to love one another in a way where His presence is felt.

If a person does not know what real love is about, the main thing the marriage might have is the application of lust rather than love in the relationship. But God builds a relationship with you so you understand how to build a marriage that's sustainable. Lusting to be with a person because of what you can get out of it will cause you to have the wrong idea of what love is. It might look like love to you, but the incorrect application of love will have you believing that because a person buys you a gift and feeds your ego, this person has your best interests at heart and loves you. Unless they are able to build from the foundation of real love—knowing who and what love is—the only thing a person can present to you is a lustful desire to be with you.

Having love for one another means that I can only treat you in a way that is pleasing to Him, and rest assured that it will be pleasing to your spouse. Marriage is a willingness to do whatever is needed to get you to the place of devotion to one another.

Family, lust is nothing like falling in love with God. Lust is never satisfied, whereas understanding His kind of love strengthens you. The love you have for Him and your willingness to receive His love grows the marriage relationship you are willing to build through love. The power of love is built through your relationship with God and continues to be developed within God. It's what's being developed inside you that causes you to look at your spouse and see Jesus.

The love the Father raised Jesus from the dead with is the same kind that will raise the love you have for Him and your spouse, and that love will give you the power to build you up in your relationship.

We ought always to thank God for you, brothers and sisters, and rightly so, because your faith is growing more and more, and the love all of you have for one another is increasing.

— – 2 THESSALONIANS 1:3

Love is what's needed to build something that's attractive to the spiritual eyes. The beautiful thing about having the right type of power in your relationship is that it gives you the ability to do loving things or act in loving ways. This power gives you the ability to direct or influence the behavior of your relationship for the better.

You must be able to look at your spouse just like the Father looks at you. The Father looks at your marriage from on high with expectation and excitement, and He knows a great marriage can come about through the love and power He provides. As a spouse, you get to speak what the spirit of God tells you to speak. Your words get to be filled with His love and power. The Father provides you with eyes of expectation and trust in your spouse, not eyes of suspicion. The Spirit who lives in you desires you to have the same type of relationship with your spouse that Jesus has with the Father and the Holy Spirit: "That they may be one, just as We are one; I in them and You in Me, that they may be perfected and completed into one" (John 17:22–23 AMP). In Him, we have the strength we need to make it through. "Though one can overpower him who is alone, two can resist him. A cord of three strands is not quickly broken" (Ecclesiastes 4:12 AMP).

When you know you are beloved, you understand that you cannot waste your time believing the negative ideas others have about marriage instead of the promises God has given you. Do not allow what a person thinks about you to stop you from being the person God has made, one who knows he or she is created to invoke change. God the Father gave you a commandment not to trust everything people may say pertaining to your marriage and its future. Your relationship needs your full commitment to you being the person who knows they are beloved. If you do not believe you are beloved, you will not do your part in turning your marriage into a place where you feel loved. Just like Jesus, you need to not carry out your own will and purpose, which can be swayed by the influence of others but do the will and purpose of Him who sent you (see John 6:38).

You must always take ownership of the choices you make. You decide if you are or are not going to include Him in your marriage. How you look at your situation is more important than what you do in it, even though that's important too, so when you look at your spouse through God's eyes, what you see will motivate you to be the light that reflects God's heart of love. Becoming good at anything big requires you to become great at the small things. The Father desires for you to be a great spouse. He does this by identifying your small steps of progress to encourage you and prevent you from becoming frustrated with the process. Be pleased with your willingness to take baby steps. Over time you are developing your love and having an appreciation for where you find yourself in your marriage.

Your marriage is also based on friendship. As close friends, you know that it does not matter what comes your way; you are both going to be there when it counts. You should have a committed heart, one that solidifies your promises to your spouse that you are in it together. Your spouse can feel secure knowing there isn't anything that is going to push you toward someone else and away from them, just like Ruth promised her mother-in-law, Naomi. "Ruth said, 'Do not urge me to leave you or to turn back from following you; for where you go, I will go, and where you lodge, I will lodge. Your people will be my people, and your God, my God'" (Ruth 1:16 AMP). When you say your marriage vows, you are saying, "I go where you go, I do what you desire to do, I go where you desire to go, and only when you or I am laid to rest will I be released from this marriage." Your spouse never has to worry about your commitment to love.

As a friend, I am excited to be in a relationship with my spouse. I know and trust that our hearts are attracted to one another. The attraction of the heart comes from God's love and carries His power and authority. No single person can have love greater than love Himself, so we must have His love in us to love well. Understanding all that we can about why we are in a relationship with each other as close, committed friends matters. The bond that we have should be so strong that we are each willing to lay down our life for our friend. "No one has greater love [nor stronger commitment] than to lay down his own life for his friends" (John 15:13 AMP). Giving up your life for someone is not something that should be taken for granted. It contains the correct type of motivation—love. When you have it, you feel like you have an S on your chest, and you are willing to die for your spouse. Your willingness to do this comes from understanding your role as a friend. "What a friend we have in Jesus, all our sins and griefs to bear!"[2]

Within your relationship, your being led by Jesus will be attractive to your spouse. My recommendation is that you learn how to be led by the spirit of God so that your spouse will not be afraid to follow you. As long the goodness of God remains as the foundation of your relationship, and you always choose holiness, your spouse will trust you. "You have an anointing from the Holy One [you have been set apart, specially gifted and prepared by the Holy Spirit], and all of you know [the truth because He teaches us, illuminates our minds, and guards us from error]" (1 John 2:20 AMP). You are on a love mission, and you are trying to live that in your marriage. This means that you are going to love your spouse the way that God would have you love them.

You love your spouse because you understand the potential of the marriage. Your marriage is like a lemon and tea—you want to squeeze the lemon (God's provision for marriage) to get the right flavor in your tea (a strong, love-filled marriage). The more you squeeze, the more you fill your marriage. I am here to encourage you to squeeze all the God juice into your marriage. We serve a God who replenishes us; He is a provider, and He will continue to keep your marriage strong, filling it with the right contents and flavor. He will not allow it to go dry.

Hopefully, you are starting to understand the importance of establishing a foundational love that starts with the relationship you have with God. When you find yourself in a situation where you are doing something that's not pleasing to God, He is the only one who can get to the heart of your situation. And when He does, you must be willing to be pulled out of your situation. "Let not steadfast love and faithfulness forsake you, bind them around your neck; with them on the tablet of your heart" (Proverbs 3:3 ESV).

LOVE YOUR MARRIAGE

We have to know that God the Father loves us and knows what's best for us. He is not a Father who rules through enforcement but one who rules through love. God so loves us that He made a choice to give up His Son to redeem the world back to Himself. Even though it was a hard decision for God to allow His Son to go through this, He did not make this decision based on emotions.

Making an emotional decision is one of the worst choices a person can make because it usually means we do not think about the consequences attached to the decision. This is why a person should change their mind about the goal being to seek happiness in a relationship. God said that we should find joy—unspeakable joy— and not happiness in a marriage.

Remain in My love [and do not doubt My love for you]. If you keep My commandments and obey My teaching, you will remain in My love, just as I have kept My Father's commandments and remain in His love. I have told you these things so that My joy and delight may be in you, and that your joy may be made full and complete and overflowing.

— – JOHN 15:9–11 (AM)P

You can love being a part of your marriage so much that you cannot speak anything that will cause it to shift in the wrong direction. God desires that we make deci-sions like He does—by removing the emotion out of the decision-making process. Just imagine if God had made His emotions the main part of His deci-sion-making; I believe that He would have never come down to the earth in order for us to have access to the kingdom. If that decision had not been made, where would we be today? Instead, God made His decision based on the love and joy He has for us. "I came that they may have and enjoy life, and have it in abun-dance [to the full, till it overflows]" (John 10:10 AMP). He knows what's needed in our lives. This is the type of mentality we should aspire to have.

Your strong belief in God will grant you access to His joy, and you can rejoice with the person you are connected to. You have been anchored in your marriage by God to God, and He offers no way of escape. This provides both of you with security, knowing that even if you desire anything that will pull you in the wrong direction, He will pull you back to righteousness. Celebrating your marriage helps you focus on what you love being a part of and who you have an appreciation for being with. God so loves you! Understand that it is possible to be in a marriage with someone for eternity and enjoy every moment of it when you're one with Him. He is consistently dropping nuggets of wisdom that motivate you to have a deeper relationship with your spouse, the one God has placed in your life.

Having a love relationship with God is a beautiful thing because He guides you in how to conduct yourself in your marriage. You have been given an opportunity to think differently about what you have. There is a purpose in visualizing yourself doing significant, loving things. Learn to put into practice yourself whatever you wish your spouse would do for you. Be willing to do whatever is needed to get the most out of your relationship. See it and believe it. Travel the high road, and treat your spouse better than you are being treated. "I lay down My [very own] life [sacrificing it] for the benefit of the sheep" (John 10:15 AMP).

LOVE DEVELOPS FRUIT IN YOUR MARRIAGE

Gather up and carry out His thoughts about marriage. Visualize yourself loving with His love. Coming together and staying together is an objective of the Holy Spirit. He knows that you are better together than you can possibly be apart. The work that has been and will be invested in your marriage is not in vain. Your marriage can be a beautiful example of what real love looks like.

Love is a gift, but deep love is the fruit produced from the marriage. "Every healthy tree bears good fruit" (Matthew 7:17 AMP). People are out looking for examples of what true love looks like. They're looking to see if you are what you claim to be. Love God. Let His love fill every part of your marriage. Love your spouse with His love. Love your marriage. Grow the fruit of the

Spirit in your marriage every day, and experience the wide-ranging joy God has designed you to have together.

> The fruit of the Spirit [the result of His presence within us] is love [unselfish concern for others], joy, [inner] peace, patience [not the ability to wait, but how we act while waiting], kindness, goodness, faithfulness, gentleness, self-control.
>
> — – GALATIANS 5:22–23 (AMP)

CHAPTER 3

Purity

Observe everything that I have commanded you.
– Matthew 28:19

PURITY, noun

The condition of being pure. Specifically:

1. freedom from foreign admixture or heterogenous matter, as the purity of water, of wine, of spirit...
2. Cleanness: freedom from foulness or dirt...
3. Freedom from guilt or the defilement of sin; innocence; as purity of heart or life...
4. Freedom from any sinister or improper views; as the purity of motives or designs.

– Webster's Dictionary 1828[1]

When you love God, you are willing to do whatever He says because you trust Him, the one who sees and knows all things, the one who "causes all things to work together [as a plan] for good for those who love God, to those who are called according to His plan and purpose" (Romans 8:28). You trust that He knows far better than you what your marriage needs and your role in it.

You need to do things the way God has instructed you to do them. He has attached certain benefits that are connected to your obedience. He has said as long as you are doing what He has commanded you to do, there is a place in the house of God specifically designed for you. Dwelling in the house of God allows Him to work on you as you deal with each situation.

Jesus came up and said to them, "All authority (all power of absolute rule) in heaven and on earth has been given to Me.

Go therefore and make disciples of all the nations [help the people to learn of Me, believe in Me, and obey My words], baptizing them in the name of the Father and of the Son and of the Holy Spirit, teach- ing them to observe everything that I have commanded you; and lo, I am with you always [remaining with you perpetually— regardless of circumstance, and on every occasion], even to the end of the age."

— – MATTHEW 28:18–20 (AMP)

God's always with us. Why would we ever want to step out of His divine presence, protection, and blessings? When you come to a place where you make up your mind that you are going to agree with God and do what He says, your mind will relax. He is bigger than your marriage. Through obedience to Him, your marriage will become one of peace.

God is not mocked [He will not allow Himself to be ridiculed, nor treated with contempt nor allow His precepts to be scornfully set aside]; for whatever a man sows, this and this only is what he will reap. For the one who sows to his flesh [his sinful capacity, his worldliness, his disgraceful impulses] will reap from the flesh's ruin and destruction, but the one who sows to the Spirit will from the Spirit reap eternal life.

Let us not grow weary or become discouraged in doing good, for at the proper time we will reap, if we do not give in.

— – GALATIANS 6:7–9 (AMP)

Dwelling in peace does not mean that you are not going to face things that cause your flesh to tell you that you cannot handle the pressure you are facing. But you have not pledged obedience to your flesh.

When something goes wrong in a marriage, far too many people come to the incorrect place of agreement of believing that their union is too damaged to continue. The will of God for your marriage is to have you relax your mind in Him. Settle within your sprit that the seed planted in your marriage on your wedding day is a seed that's built upon a future planned by God. Based on His history established in His Word, we know that anything that comes from Him is connected to a requirement. When we fulfill the order and carry out the assignment God has commanded, we reap heavenly rewards, including a fulfilling marriage.

Do not be like the many people who don't understand how God establishes life and blessing—they have theories about the possibility of any marriage working out, but the Word has communicated that we can place our faith in the God who is committed to bring about peace in our marriage, and in His strength, we can do whatever He says to accomplish it.

GOD'S DIRECTION

If you're going to do whatever God says, you need to know the Word and recognize the voice of the Holy Spirit. Recognize that it is not about you; it's about the source you are receiving from to produce the power that's needed. Once you have what you need, you will see your life Illuminate and be an example for others. Being an example for others will motivate them to inquire about your source of power that brings so much joy to your marriage.

When someone enquires about your marriage, it means that in their eyes, they can clearly see joy has been provided, the direction of your marriage is well-defined in your mind, the instruction is on time, and you enjoy being with your spouse. You can share your source with them. The beautiful thing about this source, God, is that He will not hold back what's needed for your marriage. He knows what you need to be prepared for every moment. He's designed you to continue to grow your relationship. He'll show you things from the inside out.

There are some basics God has given us in His Word for how we should act in marriage (and in our relationship with Him):

1. A covenant is a solemn promise and a binding agreement (Genesis 6:18). Honor and obey the terms of the covenant, and blessings will abound (Genesis 7:12–15; 32:29).
2. Remain faithful to each other sexually (Hebrews 13:4).
3. Be intimate with each other regularly (1 Corinthians 7:1–4).
4. Husband, love your wife like Christ loves the church (Ephesians 5:25).
5. Wife, respect your husband (Ephesians 5:33).
6. Be humble, gentle, patient, and kind with each other (Ephesians 4:2–3).
7. Do not be harsh with each other (Colossians 3:18–19).

"Everything that the Lord has said we will do, and we will be obedient." ... The Lord your God is a merciful and compassionate God; He will not fail you, nor destroy you, nor forget the covenant with your fathers which He swore to them.

— – EXODUS 24:7; DEUTERONOMY 4:31 (AMP)

In showing you things from His perspective, God is identifying specific things about your marriage so you can have a true understanding of what's required to have a God-led marriage—actions created by God for His enjoyment in seeing you build something strong together. Because He is the creator of the marriage, He is going to help you deal with anything that will come.

You must have a personal relationship with God and see, hear, and know what He does. As your teacher and guide, the Holy Spirit is focused on your well-being. "The Helper (Comforter, Advocate, Intercessor—Counselor, Strengthener, Standby), the Holy Spirit, whom the Father will send in My name [in My place, to represent Me and act on My behalf], He will teach you all things" (John 14:26 AMP). We must develop our spiritual ear to be able to hear what the Holy Spirit is communicating. Jesus showed us how to cultivate our relationship with Him, and when we do, we have a better relationship with one another.

DO THE RIGHT THING

Goodness is within you, and it's not a mere passive quality; it's the deliberate preference of right over wrong, the firm and persistent resistance of all moral evil and the choosing of all moral good. Holiness is the cornerstone that's needed to build an efficient marriage relationship. Building your marriage off the cornerstone of goodness is the prerequisite to becoming something conceivable.

You were born into sin, which means that you did not have to learn how to pick up destructive habits; however, this also means that you did not have to learn how to reject God. You are a human being living on this earth and trying to live it to the best of your abilities. The goodness of God that lives within you communicates with you in an attempt to get you to do His will because this is what drives you into His goodness. God is devoted to you. He has authority over love and promises, and He keeps His end of His agreements. He's our role model for love and faithfulness. Be true to your relationship with Him and express your love to Him through your actions, and you'll rest in His goodness.

God the Father understands how and why you were created. I believe that because He knows you, He understands what you are and are not capable of doing. Your appreciation for what He has done in your life is expressed by your commitment to never quit on Him. When things get hard, push yourself to be more than a conqueror: "In all these things we are more than conquerors and gain an overwhelming victory through Him who loved us [so much that He died for us]" (Romans 8:37 AMP). This is what the Father looks for—He wants to see if you can recognize His DNA in you.

The Father's DNA does not contain any fear. His Spirit in you provides an infinite amount of power and love. He has given you the freedom to move as you please in this love, but moving as you please within a relationship does not mean that you are not accountable. You must still do the things you are supposed to do. Roaming free means that He trusts that you are going about things in the right way so your marriage can profit from them and grow richer and deeper. I encourage you to be persistent in taking ownership of your actions. Have the type of love affair with Him that will impact your marriage every day. Some days, you'll have to fight to do the right thing, but "thanks be to God, who gives us the victory [as conquerors] through our Lord Jesus Christ" (1 Corinthians 15:57 AMP).

When it pertains to your relationship with God, there is only one way to do anything, and that way is God's way. The reason why people have problems and issues in their marriage is that they choose the philosophy of "as good as" instead of "what God requires." And when you ask them for advice, all they desire for your relationship is that it's on the same level or worse than theirs. Comparing the two is a distinct conflict between the spirit and the flesh, and the final decision falls on you: Will you choose good enough or God's best? You have control over what will eventually take place in your life. You have dominion and authority on this earth, but you also have consequences associated with your decisions. You want to make sure that each decision is connected to something that will benefit you, not result in negative consequences. Be mature and make choices that benefit both you and your spouse.

Sin can be like a controlled substance. Your nature is going to be affected by that gravitational pull that tries to control your life, and if you want to act like a child, you'll get upset over not being able to have what you desire. Not everything has to always go your way. Make your decisions from the position of love. When you choose to do things God's way, you can have confidence in knowing that situations have no choice but to turn out in your favor and for your good.

Our heavenly Father looks at how we handle things to see if we are going to respond maturely in love or out of fleshly frustration. We must walk in the Spirit and control our flesh. The flesh daily tries to set us up to focus more on the natural than the spiritual things in life. We must remember that the spiritual man on the inside is more important than the natural man who is seen on the outside, and we need to only feed the spiritual one.

Do not be afraid of putting in the work to help make your relationship better. Put your hands to the plow. Do your research on things that will make your marriage- earning potential go up and do them. Always do what's right.

You shall do what is right and good in the sight of the Lord, so that it may be well with you and that you may go in and possess the good land which the Lord swore to [give] your fathers, by driving out all your enemies from before you, as the Lord has spoken.

— – DEUTERONOMY 6:18–19 (AMP)

HOLINESS

When you have a holy marriage built on the foundation of love, you are in a marriage that is whole and complete, elevated, and approved by God. If God's way of marriage is valuable to you, you daily make a choice to stay in that place of blessing and speak life into it.

"Holy, holy, holy is the Lord Almighty; the whole earth is full of his glory" (Isaiah 6:3). With God being holy and being a God who establishes marriages, He places His imprint upon your unique marriage so you can identify what makes your marriage effective. God positions Himself in your marriage so that you are always required to move forward together into more of His love with consistency and force. For your marriage to be successful, you must always be aware of the importance of identifying any personal change needed for you to be fulfilled in your marriage. When God is your guide, and you obey, He will ensure that all your desires are met in your marriage. Spouses in marriages built upon God's holiness are open to what is possible. Identifying that you are part of a holy marriage is linked to how you go about choosing what you build it with.

Sanctification places a spiritual guard at the gate of your marriage that prevents the enemy from getting in and challenges your desire for stepping out. Be someone who is satisfied with what you have. Understand how you should conduct yourself. Whenever a thought comes into your mind regarding breaking your vow between you and the Lord, allow the spirit of God to remind you of what is important. Allow yourself to see what will come to pass if you follow through with a poor decision. Being able to see in advance the consequences of your actions will cause you to rethink that action, especially if doing it will break up your home and bring you into a place where you cannot have peace. Because the enemy is in a place of turmoil, he desires your marriage to experience what he is experiencing. Being satisfied with what you have gives you the courage to reject the enemy's proposals and follow the plan that will bless your marriage.

Be sober-minded [be sensible, wake up from your spiritual stupor] as you ought, and stop sinning; for some [of you] have no knowledge of God [you are disgracefully ignorant of Him, and ignore His truths].

— – 1 CORINTHIANS 15:34 (AMP)

You can gain a blessing as big as what you open your spiritual heart to. People who are successful in life master their ability to focus on what they are able to produce. Be willing to purge yourself of everything you don't need in your marriage. Be a vessel of holiness that contains God's power and love, and only carry the things that are needed. The spirit of God is the sail that's attached to your vessel, capturing the winds of God that push you to your destination. You are needed for the cargo you carry, not only for your life but also for the lives attached to yours.

You are a vessel created by God to carry gifts like righteousness, faith, love, peace and joy—all building materials being constructed into a temple of marriage that's pleasing to the sight of God. If the items used to build it are the incorrect components, the temple will not be strong enough to resist the forces that come against it. Disparaging ideas can hover around your mind, looking for an opportunity to be implemented in your marriage, and if you let them in, you'll quickly recognize by their fruit that they are not from God.

Before you implement anything in your marriage, I recommend that you create a filtration system that guards you both against destructive ideas. The Holy Spirit Himself (your strong temple) is your most powerful filtration system. He'll send you notifications of anything He deems as beneficial or detrimental to your relationship. He can do this because He has the ability to stand tall, see things at a distance, and warn you in advance. Your marital tower is only built up based on the implementation of the correct ideas.

The way towers were built back in the 1900s is not the way they are being built today. Based on the wisdom that has been obtained over the years, our thinking has evolved on what the best way of building a tower is, and now new practices are in place that are followed on a consistent basis. Do not do the ordinary things; do the things that make your marriage extraordinary by listening to the Holy Spirit and doing whatever He asks. And in everything you do, do it to the best of your ability.

Whatever you do [no matter what it is] in word or deed,
   do everything in the name of the Lord Jesus [and in

dependence on Him], giving thanks to God the Father through Him.

— – COLOSSIANS 3:17 (AMP)

HOLINESS KEEPS US IN A POSITION OF AUTHORITY

Jesus went into the wilderness because God told Him to. It was there that He used the authority of the word "no," no matter how badly He wanted to eat, have all the kingdoms of the world before His time, or prove He was God (Luke 4:1–13).

Satan: Command this stone to turn into bread. Jesus: NO!

Satan: Worship me, and I'll give you all the kingdoms of the inhabited earth. Jesus: NO!

Satan: Throw yourself off the pinnacle of the temple.

Jesus: NO!

"When the devil had finished every temptation, he [temporarily] left Him until a more opportune time" (v. 13). When we say no to sin, the devil leaves us alone for a while. He doesn't stop, but he recognizes when trying to tempt us is a waste of his time.

When Jesus came out of that time in the desert, He was walking in authority, and everyone knew it. "They were surprised [almost overwhelmed] at His teaching because His message was [given] with authority and power and great ability" (Luke 4:32). Jesus lived in this world in a human body, but He functioned in the authority that was given to Him by His Father. That authority had people amazed only because they lacked belief in what they were able to do. It's the same when it comes to your marriage, so don't lack belief in what God is able to do. Use your authority.

Understand that you possess the same human body and authority to live in a marriage that produces joy. Marriage was created by God for your enjoyment and His good pleasure. God is pleased when we show Him that we trust Him, we have expectations of His power to make our marriage good, and we are determined to live this life for Him in obedience and holiness. These are the main reasons we should put forth our best effort in making our marriage the best it can be.

In knowing that you have the upper hand in Jesus, you know how important it is to follow the correct instructions for your marriage. Know that issues, concerns, disputes, problems, and the like are examples of negative things that cannot take up permanent residence in your marriage. You are in a relationship with someone who is willing to build on God's foundation of love with you. Together, you can rejoice and smile when you know that the Adversary is out to destroy you, be- cause he does not possess enough power to accomplish his goal.

NEVER GIVE AWAY THE GATE CODE

Your marriage is guarded and protected from outside forces that do not possess the code to gain access. If they had it, they'd try to destroy your marriage. For example, a spouse finds out that infidelity has taken place in their marriage. The only way infidelity could have taken place is because someone gave another person access to something they were never supposed to have access to.

Dr. Shirley Glass, one of the world's leading experts on infidelity, has summarized her insight on how to avoid it:

1. *Maintain appropriate walls and windows.* Keep the windows open at home. Put up privacy walls with others who could threaten your marriage.

2. *Recognize that work can be a danger zone.* Don't lunch alone or take coffee breaks with the same person all the time. When you travel with a coworker, meet in public rooms, not in a room with a bed.

3. *Avoid emotional intimacy with attractive alternatives* to your committed relationship. Resist the de- sire to rescue an unhappy soul who pours his or her heart out to you.

4. *Protect your marriage by discussing relationship issues at home.* If you do need to talk to someone else about your marriage, be sure that person is a friend of the marriage. If the friend disparages marriage, respond with something positive about your own relationship.

5. *Keep old flames from reigniting.* If a former lover is coming to the class reunion, invite your partner to come along. If you value your marriage, think twice about having lunch with an old flame.

6. *Don't go over the line when you're online with internet friends.* Discuss your online friendships with your partner and show him/her your email if he/she is

interested. Invite your partner to join in your correspondence so your internet friend won't get any wrong ideas. Don't exchange sexual fantasies online.

7. *Make sure your social network is supportive of your marriage.* Surround yourself with friends who are happily married and who don't believe in fooling around.

– Dr. Shirley Glass[2]

As a couple, you should decide on what ideas and opinions you are willing to accept in your relationship. The things that you accept should be examined and analyzed to see if they are welcome in your marriage. A person who respects and understands they're responsible for protecting their marriage understands that if they have a conflict in their marriage, they need to have a conversation with their spouse in order to come up with a plan that protects them both against this force that's out to destroy the marriage.

Be sober [well balanced and self-disciplined], and be alert and cautious at all times. That enemy of yours, the devil, prowls around like a roaring lion [fiercely hungry], seeking someone to devour.

— – 1 PETER 5:8

Guard your marriage like you guard your heart. Not everyone should be able to have access to your heart be- cause you understand the value of your emotional health. Accepting the wrong thing should never be an option. According to the world's perspective, the odds are against you having a successful marriage. Be prepared in knowing that things are going to come against you, but know that you are well equipped to stand in the face of adversity and tell it where to go.

Only average people think that they cannot build and grow their marriage into something that's indestructible. Learn how to stand and not waddle in your marriage. A person who takes a stand for their marriage establishes it as a secure place for the family to dwell. There is nothing like having a living, functional, vibrant, and emotionally healthy relationship with someone who has an appetite to stay in the fight.

Having an appetite means you crave something that you think has the capacity of satisfying what you desire. Examine the thing you desire very seriously. If you do not find a way to satisfy that urge in God, you will be vulnerable to being pulled away from the place that's designed to keep you safe. Learn how to develop a mentality in which the only person who can satisfy your desire is your spouse. When you tell one another you find full satisfaction in the other's presence, you will start believing these things. Then, when the enemy comes in like a flood, you can exhibit your agreed-upon standard and reject the temptation that's out to destroy you.

When a flood occurred, the torrent burst against that house and yet could not shake it, because it had been securely built and founded on the rock.

— – LUKE 6:48 (AMP)

The enemy tries to deluge you and your spouse with the idea that your desires cannot be met within your marriage. But when you have built up your spiritual immune system in God's truth, you can reject the temptation of moving outside your marriage to satisfy an ungodly desire.

HUMILITY

We should be sober-minded in making decisions—reasonable, self-controlled, and self-possessed—just like God. Know how much God wants your marriage to have your undivided attention, and be humble enough to accept that His ways are better than yours. Knowing what your marriage is established on is key, and following God's rules for marriage must come before your own ideas. "As they were going along the road, ... Jesus said to him, "No one who puts his hand to the plow and looks back [to the things left behind] is fit for the kingdom of God" Luke 9:57, 62 AMP). The mission of marriage— doing what you are called to do— takes precedence. Don't think you know better, and look back.

If you do something you know is not right, be mature and humble about it. Admit to your loved one your error. Your obedience in your marriage is far more important to your Father than anything else you could think. Do- ing what's required of you places your flesh under the control of the spirit of God and the understanding of who is in charge. Put your marriage in a position of having a do-or-die mentality.

Do everything you possibly can do to allow the spirit of God to develop your marriage. Know that God is paying close attention to see if you are implementing the correct things in your relationship. He will call you out when He notices you dwelling in a place outside of the boundaries that He expected you to stay inside.

> The Lord will tear down the house of the proud and arrogant (self-righteous), but He will establish and protect the boundaries [of the land] of the [godly] widow.
>
> — – PROVERBS 15:25 (AMP)

> The [boundary] lines [of the land] have fallen for me in pleasant places; indeed, my heritage is beautiful to me.
>
> — – PSALM 16:6 (AMP)

The place that's designed for you is a place that has been prepared for you. The question that you have to answer for yourself is, are you ready to occupy your land? You are generously outfitted to handle the responsibility that comes with marriage. Will you receive His gift in humility?

Some claim that you will always find one spouse is more engaged than the other in the relationship, but I believe that some spouses might appear less engaged, but in reality, they feel as if they have to always be on the defensive. They haven't learned humility yet—the art of not thinking less of themselves and thinking of themselves less. Because of a lack of understanding of how to be "meek and holy," a person feels they must be constantly on guard. They need to learn how to be assured in who they are in the marriage, then believe that the marriage is going to eventually mold into shape. This molding of the marriage takes shape by remaining calm and trusting that what's surrounding your marriage will keep your relationship together.

DON'T GET DISCOURAGED AT DOING THE RIGHT THING

I encourage you to take the time to think about the things you have done badly in your marriage. I believe you will find you could have made better choices, done things differently, or said things a different way. It is essential to not miss out on the opportunity of getting better. Spiritual improvement and peace of mind are built around your desire to understand you are more than an overcomer. There is only one God who knows all things. He has never made a mistake, and He can show you a better way next time.

Doing things to the best of your ability means that you are not going to hold back from giving 100 percent. After having conversations with people who are on the verge of giving up, none have said that they gave 100 percent. They felt like there was something they could have done better. When we are comfortable with what we have, we have a tendency of not taking our relationships seriously, and we don't do all we can.

You do not know the day or the hour when you will leave this earth. The lifespan of your marriage is too short, so anything good you can do needs to be done now. "Teach us to number our days, that we may cultivate and bring to You a heart of wisdom" (Psalm 90:12 AMP). The love that the spirit of God has for you gives you the power to make changes in your life. He can keep you from becoming settled in bad habits. You cannot be great at anything if you never work hard on it.

Making your marriage all that it can potentially be allows you to be free from being held back. It is impossible to fail at doing the things God has commanded you to do.

THE JOY OF OBEDIENCE

Being able to accomplish this has nothing to do with what you are naturally able to do, but when you have a relationship with the God of truth, He communicates what's needed every time.

> I will bless the Lord who has counseled me; Indeed, my heart (mind) instructs me in the night.
> I have set the Lord continually before me; Because He is at my right hand, I will not be shaken.
> Therefore my heart is glad and my glory [my innermost self] rejoices;
> My body, too, will dwell [confidently] in safety. ...
> You will show me the path of life;

In Your presence is fullness of joy;
In Your right hand, there are pleasures forever- more.

— – PSALM 16:7–11 (AMP), EMPHASIS MINE

Just like you want to be shown the path to life, desire to be shown the path in understanding how to enjoy your marriage. The spirit of God communicates with you and opens your mind to all His possibilities. You want to ensure you are plugged in to the Spirit so that you are always receiving the power needed to be able to meet God's expectations. If you are meeting the expectations He has of you in your marriage, I am confident that He will deal with the heart of your spouse, too, and help them to enjoy being in a marriage with you.

CHAPTER 4

Communication

If two of you agree on earth concerning anything ...
– Matthew 18:19 NKJV

COMMUNICATE, verb

1. To share in common; to participate in.
2. To impart; to bestow; to convey; ...
3. To make known; to recount; to give; to impart; as to communicate information to anyone. ...

Communicate is the more general term, and denotes the allowing of others to partake or enjoy in common with ourselves. Impart is more specific. It is giving to others a part of what we had held as our own, or making them our partners; as, to impart our feelings; to impart of our property, etc. Hence there is something more intimate in imparting intelligence than in communicating it. To reveal is to disclose something hidden or concealed; as, to reveal a secret.

– Webster's Dictionary 1913[1]

In February 2019, my parents Dennis and Amelia Nickens celebrated fifty years of marriage. I had the privilege of sitting down with them and asking them what the glue was that keeps their marriage together. They said that over the years they faced difficult times together, but their faith, their commitment to God, and their ability to communicate helped them stay together.

Like them, you will have disagreements. Sometimes you need to find a way to walk away and come back when you both have cooler heads. My parents shared that if more couples focused on finding ways to work to- gether instead of justifying their positions, we would see more people trying to work out their issues rather than trying to get out of the marriage.

HEAR THE HEART

God is always teaching us how to dialogue, and so having amazing communication with our spouse is possible. When it happens, it's like the flow of traffic that transitions in and out of a city. The key to the flow of traffic is to ensure that it is not hindered. In the same way, ideas flow in and out of the relationship between one another. We both possess ideas that we believe are in the best interest of the relationship. When your spouse communicates these ideas with you (even if you don't agree with their thoughts), God has developed your heart so you can hear their heart as they share.

Your marriage is designed as a safe place for you both. Within its walls, you should to be able to com- municate with one another about anything and every- thing and trust that, together, you can come up with good solutions for every difficulty. I understand there are some good ideas people outside the marriage can provide, but no one knows your spouse the way you do, so it makes sense that whatever you come up with will fit better with your spouse's perspective.

Jesus said that "If two of you agree on earth concerning anything that they ask, it will be done for them by My Father in heaven. For where two or three are gathered together in My name, I am there in the midst of them" (Matthew 18:19–20 NKJV). When God is the center of a marriage, two people with different opinions and ideas can come together and make decisions together as one voice—a voice that speaks for the family. This is only possible if you have honest conversations with each other, listen in order to understand the heart of the other person, and have peace as your goal.

The Creator provided us with His gift of the Holy Spirit, which is needed to ensure the survival of your relationship. With Him, you are on a straight path to all His answers to questions you're going to have. Building a relationship with Him will build the bond between you and your spouse because you'll have had a lot of practice hearing the inner communication between you and the Spirit—from His heart to yours. After hearing God, heart-to-heart communication will be the central strength of the relationship.

The objective of the Holy Spirit is to ensure that you and your spouse are able to communicate, flow in unity, and function in oneness. He knows how to deal with you better than your spouse does. He has a candid ability to show you when you are in error and to build you up when you are down. More importantly, He can bring back to your remembrance your marriage vows to each other— the promise to stay together no matter what.

The biggest struggle a relationship can face is finding out how to understand one another. Misunderstandings can potentially lead your spouse to make regretful decisions. The way you respond to things you face in life—finding solutions or reacting —is similar to the way you listen to your loved one, and that might need changing. The key to truly understanding the heart is in learning how to become an effective listener. There is value in hearing the ideas of your spouse. The Word of God tells us that you are two become one flesh" (Matthew 19:5). This means that incorporating only your ideas into marital life is merely 50 percent of God's plan for the relationship.

Presenting an idea to your spouse rather than giving a command (which both husbands and wives might try to do) provides them with an opportunity to formulate their own opinion. A spouse who finds themselves in a marriage of mutual trust believes that their spouse is not out to hurt them. You work together to build upon plans that you put together. You never devalue your spouse's ideas. The only way you are going to have an effective plan is by learning how to listen in an effective way.

You owe it to yourself to receive ideas that come from the person with your best interests at heart.

Practice listening to your spouse:

- After sharing your thoughts with your spouse, ask them to repeat to you what they understood you were saying.
- Based on what's been communicated, you will provide feedback if they misunderstood or if they have a clear understanding about what was communicated.

Part of your marriage's mission statement (more on this later) should be to base every conversation with your spouse on first being able to establish a sense of being listened to and heard. It is not an anomaly that God made men and women different, but He still made us equal. His desire is that your marriage reflect the type of relationship He has with Jesus. Jesus was always in tune with God's heart; He understood the thoughts and words communicated between them, so this is our goal in marriage, too.

Jesus is a perfect example of how to be gentle, listen to the heart, and seek understanding together. He functioned with confidence, operating from a heart of kindness.

When it comes to my parents' successful marriage, they were so committed to building up the marriage they did not view treating each other as equals as robbery. They cared about the heart. In your relationship, do you go about your day thinking that you are superior to your spouse? If you do, you will never get to the place that allows you to be united as one.

WHEN YOU DISAGREE

In your marriage, peace is obtainable not just some of the time but all the time, based on where you choose to stand and what you choose to be important. For example, let's suppose you engage in a disagreement with your spouse. All arguments are based on the involvement of two people with a difference of opinion. The place God wants to get you to is a place of peace.

In the Gospel of Mark, we read about Jesus and His process of having peace in a place of disagreement. The winds and the sea were coming against Jesus, against what He stood for. Even though all this was taking place around Him, He understood that He could not be distracted from accomplishing the goal at hand —peace. In the midst of the storm, He stood up and spoke to the thing that pressed against Him. He spoke as someone who had authority. He knew it was what was needed. He opened His mouth and said "Peace, be still!" (Mark 4:39 ESV).

When we're in the middle of a disagreement, Jesus has already given us clear instructions as to what we should do to have peace in our marriage. Once you understand what you have, you know what you need during a quarrel with your spouse—you need to be able to get to a place where you can have a conversation and not a conflict. To get to a place of peace amid a frustrating situation, speak to your spouse using specific words that can change the situation. Say, "Love, can we find a place of peace where we can understand one another?" Once this has been communicated, just be quiet and wait for the desired outcome to take place.

The Word of God shows us that peace is the presence of the Holy Spirit on the inside; that's where it starts. When you desire to have a relationship with the God of peace, know He desires to have a relationship with you, too. Let this motivate you. Power and love dwell inside His peace. Throughout every season of marriage, we know we'll face controversial things, but peace has instant success by way of knowing how to deal with every situation. Peace is wisdom. Peace is always present; we just have to know the characteristics of peace and how to activate it.

To have a healthy marriage, you're required to understand the person you are with. Are you willing to be there with him or her, no matter what, and to give up anything that will cause confusion and disagreements? Are you willing to fight for peace? The amazing thing about being in a healthy relationship is that both parties have a heart willing to learn and grow from each other. It's not all about you. It's about you being willing and open to always hear from the blessing of your spouse's words. When you see them as a blessing, you understand that it becomes less about who you are currently and more about your development. Are you willing to learn how to communicate in peace?

Are you willing to grow and mature into the person your heavenly Father would have you be? It is never about what you can receive from the marriage that blesses you. It is what you invest in the marriage and in how much you trust Him to lead you in the right direction. Place your trust in the one who created you. He will ensure you are meeting your spouse's needs in the marriage. Do not place added pressure on your marriage by trying to control a discussion to go your way instead of bringing it to a place of agreement.

Being able to flow together is going to require that both parties be willing to put their guard down and embrace one another's perspective. We should always lift each other up, not try to degrade each other, and we can only treat each other in ways that please our heavenly Father. In everything you do, do what you are doing for the purpose of your Father being pleased with your efforts.

When we place things in their proper place of importance, we can function at the correct level in our marriage and view each situation from the correct perspective. Our position of humility and kindness, with the goal of mutual peace in our marriage, is key.

Comfort each other and edify one another, just as you also are doing. And we urge you, brethren, to recognize those who labor among you, and are over you in the Lord and admonish you, and to esteem them very highly in love for their work's sake. Be at peace among yourselves.

Now we exhort you, brethren, warn those who are unruly, comfort the fainthearted, uphold the weak, be patient with all.

See that no one renders evil for evil to anyone, but always pursue what is good both for yourselves and for all.

— – 1 THESSALONIANS 5:11–15 (NKJV)

Naturally, nothing supersedes your position in Him spiritually. Your heavenly Father desires that you and your spouse be intertwined as one in everything you do. The way this happens is by getting into agreement with Him and allowing Him to be the one in charge of each situation. Always communicate from the perspective of desiring understanding, with the goal of peace versus being right about the situation.

THE CORRECT WAY TO DISAGREE

It's not a matter of if but when you have a disagreement, so it makes sense to learn early on how to discuss your differences of opinion God's way. There is an effective way to have a disagreement, and your discussions can be pleasing to the heavenly Father.

The word *disagreement* is defined as "to fail to accord; not to agree; to lack harmony; to differ; to be unlike; to be at variance" (Webster's 1913). When you choose to go in the opposite direction of your spouse and argue, you go against the standard of God for unity. I believe that if you are able to look at a disagreement through the correct lens, you will be able to have a disagreement in a healthy way.

One way to start any discussion well is to believe that your spouse has your best interest at heart when you have a difference of opinion. They are not sharing their opinion to attack you but because they trust you to understand. Believing this makes you focus more on working things out together than walking away.

During any disagreement with your spouse, you need to be an

effective listener. You have the ability to restrain your negative reactions and open your heart to hear what your spouse is communicating to you. Your spouse might have an opinion that does not agree with your thoughts, but lashing out is not effective. I recommend that you humble yourself and find out why your spouse views the situation this way. Only children desire to dominate a situation in order to control an individual. Your spouse has been blessed with a brain, and spouses can think for themselves. Don't assume that only your perspective makes sense.

1. Whenever there is an issue you need to talk about, communicate with them that you would like to have a conversation with them about it. Doing this lets them know that you seek to dialogue about it and not present a monologue.
2. Let your spouse know that you are going to focus on the issue at hand and you agree to not bring any past issues into the discussion.
3. The objective of any disagreement should be to get you and your spouse to a place of understanding.

Doing this, I believe, will bring about some form of understanding between you both. Only people who are seeking to improve their relationship are willing to take information that is beneficial.

Communication is like a receiver. Learn to be receptive to what's being communicated. Regurgitating your thoughts helps build an effective back-and-forth discussion. Lacking understanding about a spouse's communication thoughts is like a ripple that has the potential of developing into a tidal wave—and it can become a huge block. Work hard on listening and understanding. Your job is to know and understand what's going on in your spouse's mind and become obsessed with winning for the team you have become in your marriage. Winning in your marriage is not about who is right and who is wrong; it is about emphasizing and always doing the things that are important and essential.

Next time you're having a discussion with your spouse, remember the goal is to be able to come to a place of understanding followed by agreement so that you can deal with the situation together. Operate from a place of understanding, and you will be amazed at how you and your spouse are able to function at the same level.

PEACE IS AN AGREEMENT

All aspiring entrepreneurs start with an idea introduced in their minds they then run with, and from that idea, other things come into place to help develop that idea. Your spouse can develop your marriage with you. He or she is designed to do this, but your idea of marriage must come to a place of agreement together. You must both understand that you are each part of your combined idea of marriage. If you are unable to come to this position of understanding, it is not possible to come to a place of agreement in most discussions.

Businesses have been destroyed because of its people not

agreeing with an idea. One of the most important things about being in a successful marriage with someone is being able to come to a place of agreement with them often. "Every kingdom divided against itself will be ruined, and every city or household divided against itself will not stand" (Matthew 12:25). When your goal is to have peace in your marriage, you are obligated to come to a state of harmony on each issue if you wish to always effectively move forward in your marriage. Having this goal removes any options available that would prevent you from working together.

The thought of working together with the love of your life should put your mind at ease, not inspire anxiety. If you live in a home where agreement and peace dwell, you live in a home where you can relax and enjoy one another. The Father wants us to always be able to function from and to a place of peace, so it should be a permanent goal for you, especially in your honesty with each other about what you think and how you feel about anything that affects your relationship. He does not want your relationship to be hindered by disagreements because he wants you to keep moving forward in oneness so you can be more effective together.

Do not concern yourself with what your spouse is and is not doing. The only things you should concern yourself with are the issues going on in you that you can control. Stressing over the things they are doing is only going to cause consistent issues to arise.

If there are issues that need to be addressed, you need to have hope that your spouse is open to hearing your heart. Communicate with faith, making sure that what you are communicating is said in the right tone. This opens up the conversation and brings about understanding. When your spouse communicates their thoughts pertaining to the issues in your marriage, be thankful that a breakthrough is about to take place, and they are willing to work on improving the relationship.

You'll only find out what's important to your spouse when you ask and listen. From this position, everything in the relationship is put into perspective. Your spouse is not the one you should be fighting against but the one you are working with. They're the person who is well equipped to be an equal contributor to the relationship. They have some of the tools needed to be able to get the job done. It's a beautiful thing to be able to see the wisdom of God manifested when you listen and understand.

Transitioning from agreement to agreement throughout the years of being together fosters the best relationship possible. Put the time into learning about the tools of agreement God has given you both. They're designed for working on areas that require understanding, which will in turn nurture your marriage to where it has no walls or limits.

Who is wise and understanding among you? Let them show it by their good life, by deeds done in the humility that comes from wisdom. But if you harbor bitter envy and selfish ambition in your hearts, do not boast about it or deny the truth. Such "wisdom" does not come down from heaven but is earthly, unspiritual, demonic. For where you have envy and selfish ambition, there you find dis- order and every evil practice.

But the wisdom that comes from heaven is first of all

pure; then peace-loving, considerate, submissive, full of mercy and good fruit, impartial and sincere. Peacemakers who sow in peace reap a harvest of righteousness.

— – JAMES 3:13–18

A marriage that has no limits is like a deep ocean. Wise discussions and mutual insight will draw out items that don't belong in this place of love because of your oneness. "The purposes of a person's heart are deep waters, but one who has insight draws them out" (Proverbs 20:5). There are treasures deep inside your spouse that your understanding and insight can bring to the surface, "that [you] may be encouraged in heart and united in love, so that [you] may have the full riches of complete understanding, in order that [you] may know the mystery of God, namely, Christ, in whom are hidden all the treasures of wisdom and knowledge" (Colossians 2:2–3).

The peace in your marriage as well as your willing- ness to grow will help you to be a blessing to others. Through prayer and studying the Word, you are taught by God about your marriage all the time. Over time, you will develop skills to understand one another better. Listening to understand provides you with information about what's going on in your spouse rather than you trying to pull information out of them. It is much easier to have your spouse give you information in a place of trust and peace instead of fighting with them over the information you desire.

We continually ask God to fill you with the knowledge of his will through all the wisdom and understanding that the Spirit gives.

— – COLOSSIANS 1:9

If any of you lacks wisdom, you should ask God, who gives generously to all without finding fault, and it will be given to you.

— – JAMES 1:5

Applying wisdom means you have learned how to speak things that are positive in nature. You know how to focus on the good in your marriage and your combined strengths, and together, you use that to get through each issue as it arises. There are going to be times when you struggle to get to the place of agreement. Over time, though, you become wiser, and you learn how to present information in humility to get to a place where you can agree.

Whenever you have a disagreement, it is usually based on a misunderstanding—verbalized communication that has been missed. You and your spouse are like a pitcher and a catcher on a baseball field. The catcher communicates to the pitcher what they would like to see them throw. The trajectory of the ball will be relayed to the catcher if the signal is caught. If the information isn't caught, the catcher will go out to the mound and have a conversation with the pitcher to ensure they are on the same page when they communicate in the future. The key to the conversation isn't about pointing fingers; it's about making the appropriate adjustments and reaffirming that you are in this together.

PEACE ENDS CONFLICTS

Every summer, families take trips to different locations all over the world to spend time together and try new things, but making a decision on your destination can be stressful. You can have some great ideas on where to go and what to do and believe that your ideas are great for both of you, but it is not until you work through any conflict and come to a place of agreement on those ideas that you'll both have peace and look forward to the trip.

Your dwelling is anointed and appointed, and heavenly peace in your marriage will get you through any conflict. As you build your marriage, understand the process of applying peace in each situation that comes up, in order to allow your marriage to move forward in harmony. Communicating with your spouse in a soft tone is the answer to turning away any wrath that's trying to interrupt the building of your relationship.

> A gentle answer turns away wrath,
>> but a harsh word stirs up anger.
>> The tongue of the wise adorns knowledge,
>> but the mouth of the fool gushes folly. ...
>> The soothing tongue is a tree of life,
>> but a perverse tongue crushes the spirit.

> — – PROVERBS 15:1–2, 4 (EMPHASIS MINE)

Wrath is designed to destroy. It's able to stir up anger between you and your spouse. One of your objectives for your marriage must be to never become angry. We must learn how to deal with conflict, learn how to see the heart of the situation and learn how to apply life principles or peace to the situation in order to bring about peace. When you want to bring peace to a disagreement, speak in the opposite direction of the conflict. This will cause a sense of peace and calmness to take place, be- cause your objective is not to build upon the conflict.

It is difficult to find yourself in the will of God and lose your-self in your marriage. Settle in your heart that your spouse is not your opponent. They are created to be in your corner, to share their thoughts, to want what's best for you. They function, oper-ate, and score baskets for the team you are both on. Together, your goal of peace and your treatment of each other with kind-ness and gentleness will bring any conflict to a good resolution.

If anyone teaches a different doctrine and does not agree with the sound words of our Lord Jesus Christ [that everyone is worthy of honor and respect], and with the doctrine and teaching which is in agreement with godliness (personal integrity, upright behavior), he is conceited and woefully ignorant [understanding nothing]. He has a morbid interest in controversial questions and disputes about words, which produces envy, quarrels, verbal abuse, evil suspicions, and perpetual friction between men who are corrupted in mind and deprived of the truth.

— – 1 TIMOTHY 6:3–5 (AMP)

GENTLENESS

Settle within yourself that everything you do in your marriage is going to be done from a place of gentleness and respect. I have found that it is difficult to conduct myself in an evil way if I am focused on being gentle.

You have given me the shield of your salvation, and your right hand supported me, and your gentleness made me great.

— – PSALM 18:35 (ESV)

Let's imagine that your child goes outside to play in the backyard. While they are playing, they lose their balance and bruise their knee. Upon hearing your child screaming, you run outside to see what has taken place. Your child explains what happened, and you process the information and do what you need to do to address the issue–the pain. After giving your child time to calm down, you bring out the first-aid kit, which contains ointment, cotton wool balls, and bandages. You gently clean the area of any blood and apply antibacterial cream and a bandage. Then you embrace your child from the position of gentleness—you let them know that everything is going to be okay.

Gentleness is created to be a strong hand with a soft touch. It is a compassionate, loving approach concerning others' weaknesses and constraints. Communicating in gentleness means you speak from a position of truth, sometimes even awkward truth, but you guard your tone so it can be well received. Not knowing how to implement gentleness will cause further pain. Imagine if you did not have a heart of gentleness when it came to your injured child. You might have been angry with your child or laughed at the size of the scratch or rolled your eyes—all inappropriate responses that can affect your child emotionally. Your child expects you to protect them from the harmful things of this world, and every time those expectations are not met, your child becomes more distant and trusts you less. It's the same way in marriage.

Help your marriage to improve by being gentle in how you treat your spouse. It is easier to catch a person with honey than it is with vinegar. One thing your marriage needs is a consistent dosage of vitamin G (gentleness). Vitamin G consists of words softly spoken but not weak, a temper that's mild-mannered but not timid, a disposition that is sweet but not unattractive, and thoughtfulness in your expectations but not limited.

Gentleness is an action word. It requires that you act for the purpose of making your relationship better. Have the right kind of attitude, as this affects your altitude. Be willing to deal with pain with gentleness. Fight for the marriage you dream of. This attitude is within you. You contain skills to help make your marriage alive and whole. Use them to grow your marriage and cause your spouse to see the gifts God has invested in you in use. Gentleness will reveal all of God's goodness inside you.

Choosing gentleness will change your love for the better. You will become able to reveal a heart that's soft, a mind that expands, and a temperament that's under control. You are someone with some amazing positive and very attractive qualities, so let God fill your heart with His gentleness and promote peace in your home. Let God have your heart so your spouse can have all your heart too.

PEACE IS A FRIEND

We meet so many people we call friends based on the relationships we have developed with them. An interpersonal bond brings you together, and you both treat it as something special. You don't take the friendship for granted. You confide with one another because you trust you are in a place where you are safe and feel at peace.

Friend

One who entertains for another such sentiments of esteem, respect, and affection that he seeks his society and welfare; a wellwisher; an intimate associate.[2]

— – WEBSTER'S 1913

Seeing your spouse as your friend is vital in creating a peaceful environment. As friends, you work together in building a relationship with one another. You strive to understand one another better. Your friendship is like two dull swords coming together with the objective of working together in order to become one sharp object. "As iron sharpens iron, so one man sharpens [and influences] another [through discussion]" (Proverbs 27:17 AMP). You can often go about becoming sharp by learning how to work through friction that shows up in areas of your marriage that need help.

"A friend loves at all times" (Proverbs 17:17). As you work together on areas that capture your attention, you will find yourselves developing a dialogue with one another that's unique to you two. Healthy dialogue with your friend is designed to help you become a perfect complement to your spouse, prepared to deal with any situation. You recognize the things that are acceptable and unacceptable within the marriage. You are honest with yourself in being willing to cut away those things that do not belong.

Trust that your relationship has been carved out of an indestructible source. It was designed and created to withstand the pressures of life. A relationship that's in sync allows you to be able to enjoy the time you spend with one another. You do not view one another as an enemy; you view each other through the clear lens of a true friend. Best friends have access to each other's thoughts and feelings, and in marriage, this goes even deeper. You get to know your spouse in a way that no other person can know them, and you are open and willingly vulnerable to being known the same way. In return, your spouse understands the importance of protecting this area of vulnerability.

Friendship requires that you be at peace with yourself in order to be the person you aspire to be, the kind of peace that places you in the correct mindset of appreciating this amazing person in your life. Once you are able to see your spouse this way and value them as such, you will understand the value of building a relationship with them. In being a best friend, you look at them differently and embrace their perspective and love differently.

Think outside the box when it comes to being best friends with your spouse. Do not accept ideas on mar- riage from people who do your relationship harm by providing you with incorrect information on what a friend and spouse should and should not do. View this as theft from the enemy, who is out to destroy any healthy relationship you desire to have.

The type of friendship you want in your marriage is one that has both parties able to see from a different perspective but walking in agreement. Any conversation with your spouse should leave them feeling that you are sold out and committed to your friendship. The friendship is valuable to you, and you have removed any doubts within yourself about it. You are down for the cause. Put in the work in being on the same team, and do not be bothered by who scored the winning basket last time. Desire to have the type of friendship with your spouse where time that you spend with them is more important than who is right and who is wrong. "Whoever is not with me is against me, and whoever does not gather with me scatters" (Matthew 12:30).

When you expect a happy future with your best friend, it will keep you excited about what God has done and what He is about to do. Yes, there are going to be times when you'll find yourself dealing with some chal- lenges, so prepare your hearts and minds together now so that you only ever act as a true definition of friend. Be consistent and always communicate with honesty and compassion. This ought to be the goal.

When my wife and I face issues within our marriage, I ask God for wisdom and try to use it. When we talk, I aim to communicate from the position of treating her in the way that I desire to be treated—as a trusted friend. The goal of addressing any issue we may face is to be able to get to the place of agreement, and the easiest way to do this is to remain calm and communicate in a way that motivates my wife to be willing to have a dialogue about the issue.

1. I let her know that the conversation I desire to have with her is about the issue and not her.
2. My goal is to get her to understand why I am feeling the way I am feeling and not let any anger jump in. Anger ruins most discussions.

3. I focus on speaking with her with respect and kindness. Poking someone in the eye makes it difficult to hear anything that you desire to communicate to them. With Jesus being the key, He helps communicate what He wants us both to hear.
4. I try to share from my heart what I really want her to hear.
5. I trust that God will provide us both with keys that will give us guidance, understanding, and a pathway to peaceful relationship.
6. I look at the bigger, long-term picture regarding this issue.

Again, I want to reinforce that getting to a peaceful place in your marriage is the place where you desire to dwell. This allows the peace of God to minister and allows you to move forward based on you being able to relax and enjoy each moment together. This peace allows the mind to process the importance of not stressing over the things that cannot be forced upon your spouse.

Even in the relationship that you have with God, He does not force His will upon you. Just like God desires for you to build a deep friendship and oneness with Him, He wants you to be able to share the same kind of oneness with your spouse.

TRUTH

Always look at things from the perspective of seeing the big picture, not the small one in front of you. Doing this builds your ability to see the long-term effects of any de- cision, and you can make better changes based on it. What is the true picture of what's being projected in a discussion? Check what you perceive or believe is true about the issue, and be willing to change your words or your mind about it based on how God sees it. Don't make up things or leave out important facts. Leaving facts out is just the same as lying, because then your spouse doesn't know the whole story. Be an honest person and keep your integrity. Your spouse needs to know that you are focused on speaking from the position of truth. This settles anything you may be struggling with.

Looking at different aspects of your marriage will cause you to develop your spiritual eye to the point where it becomes a microscope that takes a closer look at the potential of your marriage. Potential can be negative or positive, so make your marriage potential is positive by being willing to commit to self-development and true long-suffering—"bearing with one another in [unselfish] love" (Ephesians 4:2 AMP).

The interesting thing pertaining to truth is that your place of truth could be different than your spouse's. The goal is to work to the point where your understanding of truth is the same. Once you arrive at this place called truth, you will no longer try to force your truth upon them. Through wisdom and remaining calm and patient, you'll both get to the place where you can work together. Together, your marriage will stand; divided, your marriage will fall. The plan that the Father has for your marriage is for you to stand together in unity.

Desire is to come to a place of honest and healthy communication in your marriage. Work on your foundation, and do not worry about what is persecuting you. Anything worth having is worth going through. Every difficulty brings you through the process of being prepared for something that's bigger than your marriage. The beginning of your marriage is not what your marriage will look like at the end of it. Put on your hard hat, take a look at what you desire to build, and start putting in the work. When you do it the right way, you will find that your investment pays you back more than what was invested.

Truth means having no secrets. It means being real with each other and not being afraid to show the ugly sides of yourself because your love is strong and safe. It's not like you have your spouse fooled. The greatest project you will ever work on is yourself. Keep on working on yourself and the growth of your marriage, and eventually you will see it bear fruit. Trust and believe that your marriage is an opportunity of a lifetime.

The best marriage to be a part of is one in which you embrace one another's differences and treat one another well. Learn to get over the petty stuff of arguing over who is right or wrong. Be willing to get to a place where you can understand each other's perspective, ask the right questions, listen well, respond in gentleness, and make peace your goal. Become your spouse's best friend. Learning this process is not going to happen overnight. You'll have to put in the work in getting to know the person you are married to, but the rewards are great.

CHAPTER 5

Jesus, the Bridegroom

Blessed ... are the gentle [the kind-hearted, the sweet-spirited, the self-controlled].
– Matthew 5:5 (AMP)

GROOM, verb

To tend or care for.

– Webster's Dictionary 1913[1]

In 2011, at the Oscars Ceremony, five qualified actresses were nominated as finalists for the Best Supporting Actress category. Octavia Spencer's name was called out, and the first thing she did was place her hands over her face. She was so overwhelmed with joy that she needed assistance to stand on her feet. In her speech, she recog- nized the people who helped her get to that moment. She understood that the stage where she stood was not about boasting about her accomplishments, it was about being gracious and kind in the moment and being willing to lift up others.

If you want a marriage that's balanced, you must always choose kindness. This shows you value your marriage. You never do anything that would exclude your spouse because you understand the value of what they bring to the table. You appreciate all that your marriage has to offer because you are looking at your marriage through God's eyes of love.

THE KINDNESS OF JESUS

Your kindness means you never try to take ownership of anything in your marriage. You are more interested in being able to flow together. When kindness is a priority, both parties are willing to put their guard down and only treat each other in ways that please our heavenly Father. What are you doing to please your Father? Let's place importance on the right things, function at the correct level, and view situations from God's perspective. Taking this position in your marriage is key.

> Be kind and helpful to one another, tender-hearted [compassionate, understanding].
>
> — – EPHESIANS 4:32 (AMP)

Your heavenly Father desires that you and your spouse be intertwined as one in everything you do. The way this happens is that you get into agreement with Him (God), allowing Him to be the one in charge of every situation—which means your goal is to act like Je- sus every time. The kindness of Jesus means decisions are made based on what is in the best interest of the family. You both agree in the Spirit even before a discussion takes place. Look at what you have in your possession, and understand that you have the spiritual power available to transform your marriage.

> Love [that is, unselfishly seek the best or higher good for] your enemies, and do good, and lend, expecting nothing in return; for your reward will be great (rich, abundant), and you will be sons of the Most High; because He Himself is kind and gracious and good to the ungrateful and the wicked.
>
> — – LUKE 6:35 (AMP)

Incorporating the character of Jesus keeps your spouse feeling safe and secure. No matter what might happen, your spouse knows they are with someone who has a gentle heart, is not anxious, and who seeks God first. They are thankful for the things God has blessed them with.

God had you on His mind when He gave you the gift of your spouse, and seeing your spouse through His eyes encourages you to step up and do what's right. This will move you further away from dwelling on the things you did wrong before you told God He could have your whole heart and your whole life. Now you have His spirit in you, and you are unstoppable in love.

The day you said I do is the day God anointed your teammate

to be the partner you needed to grow your marriage. The day you said I do is, the day you communicated to God that you were mature enough to handle this marriage you were committing to. You willed and desired to be with your spouse for life. You chose them, and now they are in your life for the purpose of building you up and developing your strength, and vice versa. His Spirit will fill you with all you need to be the partner your spouse needs, and He will give you the energy and motivation to keep going through the process of becoming more and more like Jesus.

> Be transformed and progressively changed [as you mature spiritually] by the renewing of your mind [focusing on godly values and ethical attitudes], so that you may prove [for yourselves] what the will of God is, that which is good and acceptable and perfect [in His plan and purpose for you].
>
> — – ROMANS 12:2 (AMP)

Our heavenly Father's eyes are always gazing upon your marriage, so focus on conducting yourself in a way that's pleasing to Him. Be willing to be like Him and operate in gentleness and peace.

Just like you are one with Jesus, He has designed marriage so you are one with your spouse. Settle in your mind that your spouse is your partner and that together, you will learn each other's rhythm so you can work together. When you learn this rhythm, it will be like poetry. Once you agree to be of one mind and one spirit and to be like Jesus, you will communicate with one another with respect, kindness, and love. You'll be motivated to work hard on your marriage and learn how to trust one another—a beautiful thing.

It is virtually impossible for a marriage to continue to function without trust. Trust opens the mind to the things that are important.

THE PEACE OF JESUS

Fort Washington, Maryland, is one of the most beautiful and peaceful places to visit in all of Maryland. The national harbor is surrounded by high-end hotels, eateries, event spaces, and a mixture of people. For me, the thing that causes this place to be a place worth visiting is the peace that's associated with it. When I'm there, I'm able to sense peace form around my thoughts. As I inhale and exhale, I am free to be honest with myself, think about my dreams, and allow hope to come, and I can feel concerns from within being lifted from my shoulders. Jesus was often able to bring peace into volatile situations. Right after he was unjustly arrested, and despite His apprehension and stress, He stopped a disciple from cutting off more ears, even going so far as to heal a man's ear so peace would reign:

The men stepped forward, seized Jesus and arrested him. With that, one of Jesus' companions reached for his sword, drew it out and struck the servant of the high priest, cutting off his ear.

"Put your sword back in its place," Jesus said to him, "for all who draw the sword will die by the sword.

— – MATTHEW 26:50–52

Jesus even left peace as one of His parting gifts, calling it out as being of high importance: "Peace I leave with you; my peace I give you. I do not give to you as the world gives. Do not let your hearts be troubled and do not be afraid" (John 14:27).

Peace of mind and peace in your relationship is a requirement. Ask God for the willpower to be a peace-filled person as you move forward. God wants you to find a way to have peace with your spouse.

Do you have an expectation of what you think your marriage should look like? Were you expecting to be served and put first when you said I do? Romans 12 provides insight into how you should go about thinking about your marriage.

By the grace given me I say to every one of you: Do not think of yourself more highly than you ought, but rather think of yourself with sober judgment, in accordance with the faith God has distributed to each of you.

— – ROMANS 12:3

Live in harmony with one another. Do not be proud, but be willing to associate with people of low position. Do not be conceited. Do not repay anyone evil for evil. Be careful to do what is right in the eyes of everyone. If it is possible, as far as it depends on you, live at peace with everyone.

—VV. 16–18

Living in harmony within your marriage should be a priority. Learn to do what's right in the eyes of your loved one. When you do what is right, you will find your- self living in peace with every- one. Come to the place of agreement and accord to have a harmonious relationship: develop a rhythm that allows you to go back and forth without missing a beat, consistent, like a clock. Consistency will stop unhealthy things from entering your marriage, and you can avoid certain problems. If something happens that causes the rhythm of your marriage to skip a beat, pay attention. Learn to sit down with your spouse and discuss what it is going to take to get back on beat. This will help keep your marriage in harmony. Always do this as soon as possible. The will of the Father is for you and your spouse to be on the same sheet of music and living a marriage in harmony.

"Blessed are the peacemakers" (Matthew 5:9). When you are a person who desires peace, the Father calls you blessed because you are about to view your situation with a God kind of light—one who can see life in your marriage. Work through the blemishes of life and choose peace in your marriage. This is the heart of the Father. You draw into your marriage what you feel should be in your marriage. God wants you to know that drawing in peace matures you and causes you to influence others to believe.

Pull peace into your mind, too. It will help you understand that your spouse is more than a person just taking up space. This person is a friend who is willing to be united and work with you. God is communicating His desire that you and the love of your life dwell in peace. Your love affair with your spouse can return and grow.

THE MERCY OF JESUS

In your marriage, there will be times when you find your- self in a situation that places you in a powerful position and leaves your spouse feeling powerless. When you find yourself in this position, you need to have a heart that's merciful. When I speak of this word mercy, only those whose minds are open to the things of God are able to understand it.

The person you have committed to is a reflection of you. It is not the Father's will that you take advantage of your spouse based on them temporarily feeling disconnected from you and wronging you. It is His will that you walk softly and have leniency. Desire to understand why it is that you no longer feel connected at a heart-to-heart level with your spouse.

One thing about life that we must understand is that we go through peaks and valleys. A time and situation will come when you need the mercy of God to be placed upon you for your spouse. The Father understands these moments. His desire is to allow us to see our spouse, whom He has given us, in the way that He sees them. This does not mean that your spouse should not be held accountable for the things they have done, but God mandates mercy. You must discuss as mature adults what has happened, with the goal of coming to a place of agreement.

The Father is the one who sits on the throne of your marriage as the Righteous Judge, not you. You are in your marriage as a co-laborer with Him, and in that place, you understand that giving your spouse mercy should not be viewed as the world may view it. Having pity on him or her does not mean you are weak; it means that you have compassion for them and are willing to work toward forgiveness.

Mercy means not giving someone what they deserve, holding back from punishing someone who hurts you. In marriage, we hurt each other many times, especially in the early years. God says not to punish each other when this happens but to be merciful. Jesus said, "Blessed are the merciful, for they will be shown mercy" (Matthew 5:7). He had far more time for the merciful than the religious during His ministry years.

> Woe to you, teachers of the law and Pharisees, you hypocrites! You give a tenth of your spices—mint, dill and cumin. But you have neglected the more important matters of the law—justice, mercy and faithfulness. You should have practiced the latter, without neglecting the former.
>
> — – MATTHEW 23:23

Jesus was known as a man of mercy—search the word mercy in your Bible and see how many people cried out for His mercy as

He passed by. This is what your marriage should be known for also.

My father told me a long time ago that there are no perfect marriages. You are going to do things over the years that will get on each other's nerves. We have to be in the mindset that we may not be perfect, but we are willing to be perfected. Desire to have harmony within your relationship. Be like Jesus. Be kind. Be as stubborn about not getting angry as Jesus. Don't allow the devil to break the lines of communication that you have with God, primarily, and with your spouse, secondarily. When you understand a mistake has been made, it makes it easier to have compassion for your spouse. If you're struggling to forgive, the Father requires that you think about all the things He has forgiven you for. He can do His part by working on your heart as you work toward forgiveness.

Psalm 23:6 justifies the importance of having mercy in your heart. "Surely your goodness and love will follow me all the days of my life, and I will dwell in the house of the Lord forever." It's communicated without a shadow of a doubt that His goodness and mercy will be with you throughout the process. This means doing things in the way God has instructed you to do things. He has attached certain benefits connected to your obedience. He said as long as you are doing the things He has commanded you to do, there is a place in the house of God specifically designed for you. Being in the house of God allows Him to work on you as you deal with each situation.

Oh, the depth of the riches of the wisdom and knowledge of God!

How unsearchable his judgments and his paths beyond tracing out!

— – ROMANS 11:33

Do not get me wrong—no one said that this process was going to be easy. I am communicating to you that though you might find it difficult to have a heart that's willing to have mercy toward your spouse, the Father will do His part in restoring your marriage. It is the heart of the Father to not see any of His children in a place where they cannot come to a place of agreement. Recognize the purpose of the enemy—for you and your spouse to have hearts that have hardened toward each other—and resolve to give mercy and to work together in harmony.

All of us also ... were by nature deserving of wrath. But because of his great love for us, God, who is rich in mercy, made us alive with Christ even when we were dead in transgressions—it is by grace you have been saved.

— – EPHESIANS 2:3–5

WE ARE THE JOY OF JESUS

Jesus has such joy when He looks at us. "This pleasure and joy of mine is now complete" (John 3:29 AMP). Your spouse is precious, and when you can see this, it fills you with joy at the thought of spending time together. You get to celebrate what is them. To be able to view what's within this gift from God requires the joy of the one who created the gift.

> [Joy is] the passion or emotion excited by the acquisition or expectation of good; that excitement of pleasurable feelings which is caused by success, good fortune, the gratification of desire or some good possessed, or by a rational prospect of possessing what we love or desire; gladness; exultation; exhilaration of spirits.

> — – WEBSTER'S DICTIONARY 1913

Joy is a delight of the mind.

> — – JOHN LOCKE (1632–1704)

Joy is not happiness; it's not connected to circumstances or emotions. Joy is the power to be content. Joy is in him.

Every day you should communicate to God, and your spouse, something you view as being precious in them. A precious gift is something that cannot be replaced. What you communicate out of your mouth and how you conduct yourself around them will deepen the love in your marriage. The desire of your heart is to be with someone you enjoy being with, and you can make that happen by being thankful for every opportunity you have to spend time with them. "I have told you these things so that My joy and delight may be in you, and that your joy may be made full and complete and overflowing" (John 15:11 AMP). "I will see you again, and [then] your hearts will rejoice, and no one will take away from you your [great] joy" (John 16:22 AMP).

OUR HUMBLE JESUS—THE DEATH OF PRIDE

Do not merely look out for your own personal interests but also for the interests of others. Have this same attitude in yourselves which was in Christ Jesus [look to Him as your example in selfless humility], who ... emptied Himself ... by assuming the form of a bond-servant and being made in the likeness of men [He became completely human but was without sin, being fully God and fully man]. ...

He humbled Himself [still further] by becoming obedient [to the Father] to the point of death, even death on a cross. For this reason also [because He obeyed and so completely humbled Himself], God has highly exalted Him.

— – PHILIPPIANS 2:4–9 (AMP)

This life that you live has and will always deal with some form of testing in unfamiliar situations. It's like traveling to a foreign country: you find yourself in a location that has a rhythm about it that seems strange to you. For you to adjust to the rhythm, you have to be willing to let go of something from your past. If you don't, you potentially could hinder your development. This thing you must be willing to give up is called pride.Pride is a huge hindrance that has to be barred for your marriage to reach its maximum potential. Just like a plane's engineer understands what it is going to take for it to lift off, we must understand how pride will prevent a marriage from taking off.

In a healthy marriage, spouses spend time learning how to understand each other and how to serve each other. They focus on what their spouse needs, and they are willing to give up anything that will damage growth. The amazing thing about being in a healthy relationship is that you both have a heart willing to learn and grow. It's not all about me. It's about me being willing and open to hearing this blessing of a person in my life. With me seeing them as a blessing, I understand that it becomes less about who I am currently and more about my development. Are we both willing to grow and mature into the people our heavenly Father would have us be?

It is never about what I can receive from the marriage that blesses me; it is what I invest in the marriage. I trust God to lead me in the right direction. I place my trust in the one who created me. He will ensure that I am meeting my spouse's needs in the marriage. I won't add pressure to my marriage based on my desire to control my spouse. My marriage is a place of agreement. We have a commitment to peace and mutual understanding.

Being able to flow together is going to require that both parties be willing to put their guard down and be vulnerable. Embrace one another from a perspective of lifting each other up and of only treating each other in a way that pleases our heavenly

Father, not lowering each other. In everything that we do, we want our Father to be pleased with our efforts. When we place things in their proper place and make the character of Jesus our priority, we can function at the correct level together and view situations from the correct perspective. Positioning each other more highly is key. "Be devoted to one another in love. Honor one another above yourselves" (Romans 12:10).

Understand that positioning each other higher does not supersede your position in Him spiritually. Your heavenly Father desires that you and your spouse be intertwined as one in everything you do. Get into agreement with God first, and allow Him to be in charge of every situation. Then, seek to listen rather than tell your spouse how it is and how it will be.

The value of being humble is that you will be honest with yourself about any weakness you have, and you'll spend time becoming more like Jesus in these areas of your life. Have a creative mindset that's excited about paying attention to your weaknesses in order to be a better spouse. Desire to be patient with your spouse. Delight in seeking understanding. Be diligent in seeking out anything beneficial to make you a better spouse. It is not about being a perfect spouse, it is about becoming a better spouse. Your humble interaction with your spouse is seen by your heavenly Father, and He is watching to see if you are going to implement the things that you learn from listening.

You owe it to yourself to find a way of changing the direction you are going if you're being prideful and demanding instead of humble. God desires your fulfillment in your marriage, and it requires your humility to listen to Him to lead the way. Produce good fruit in your marriage by paying attention to the vision God gave you for your marriage. It is created inside you, but it will require you to put in the work for it to be revealed on the outside. Be zealous about communicating your thoughts in humility so you and your spouse can work together in bringing your thoughts to pass. As your spouse interprets their thoughts, ensure that you are open-minded and willing to hear the benefits of what they are saying. Expect to benefit from your spouse's words and input. Their input is just as valid as yours and should be given the same level of consideration as your own thoughts, just as Jesus did with His disciples. Building your marriage upon the rock of God and the character of Jesus will cause everything to work out in your favor. During the incubation period of being humble and patient, appreciate the process. It will make you a better spouse.

Your marriage is a resting place. Use wisdom when you talk. Seek out the secrets of your spouse's heart. Can they trust you with their secrets? Will you be humble and encouraging with them? You are responsible for what comes out of your mouth. Always desire to build your marriage up so you can have a relationship worth celebrating. You can enjoy being trained to be all that you can be in your marriage, and I believe that it's pleasing in the Father's sight when you do.

SELF-CONTROL

The structure of a house that's stable has all the parts working together as one.

We will grow to become in every respect the mature body of him who is the head, that is, Christ. From him, the whole body, joined and held together by every supporting ligament, grows and builds itself up in love as each part does its work.

— – EPHESIANS 4:15–16

When you have a couple working together as a single unit, there must be balance from within to understand when to step up and when to step back in your relationship. In many marriages, leadership roles switch based on how God has made you, not on your gender. Stepping up in your relationship means that you are positioning yourself in leadership because you possess the knowledge and wisdom to make a decision that will make you both better off. On the other hand, when you are taking a step back, you recognize that your spouse is in the best position to make the decision, and you are required to support the person leading. An effective leader recognizes the need for self-control regarding when to step into the role of leader and when to humbly acknowledge it's time for their spouse to lead. This requires ongoing training and continually renouncing the spirit of stubbornness. We all need our minds under the Lord's control, and our minds need to be built up with God's wise thoughts instead of our own impulsive ones.

A mind that's under control works best when it is sober and patient.

Whoever is patient has great understanding, but one who is quick-tempered displays folly.

— PROVERBS 14:29

A hot-tempered person stirs up conflict, but the one who is patient calms a quarrel.

— PROVERBS 15:18

Better a patient person than a warrior, one with self-control than one who takes a city.

— PROVERBS 16:32

Jesus had great self-control in the desert, even though Satan tried his best to pull Him away from what was right (Matthew 4). Because He has power over impulsive choices, we have access to that strength today: "No temptation has overtaken you except what is common to mankind. And God is faithful; he will not let you be tempted beyond what you can bear. But when you are tempted, he will also provide a way out so that you can endure it" (1 Corinthians 10:13).

Self-control is not going to manifest right away. It is going to take time before it can become a permanent thing in your mind and heart. Whenever you introduce a new behavior into your relationship, know that what you plan will never turn out the way you expected it to. Implementation of an agreed-upon idea is going to require work on both sides in order to have a balanced equation. This is not a Disney movie: "Let's both have self-control," she said, and suddenly, they had self-control all the time, and they lived happily ever after. No, growth is a lifelong process. Through time, you are going to make consistent adjustments as you learn how to control your thoughts, your facial expressions, and your actions. Yes, de- termine to show self-control, but also accept you'll succeed and fail as you try. You'll learn better this way.

Don't despise the small steps you take. As you manage your reactions, recognize that you're working with a small seed in the beginning. Have a system in place with your spouse so that when either of you does lose self-control, grace is ready. The relationship you have with your spouse will always need your attention if it is to grow into what you hope it will become. God has every resource you need to have a great marriage, so learn to trust the will of God when He says He wants you to control yourself. Lock into the godly ideas that should take up residence in your marriage. Having control over yourself is designed to be profitable and allows you to not be concerned about anything but the strengthening presence of God in your marriage.

> The fruit of the Spirit [the result of His presence within us] is love [unselfish concern for others], joy, [inner] peace, patience [not the ability to wait, but how we act while waiting], kindness, goodness, faithfulness, gentleness, self-control. Against such things, there is no law.

And those who belong to Christ Jesus have crucified the sinful nature.

— – GALATIANS 5:22 –24 (AMP)

Rules suffocate your relationship's ability to flourish, while His Spirit inside you makes you want to be more like Him, which automatically grows your marriage. Speak the things God has placed in your heart to speak. Love the way God would love. Act the way God would act—with patience, love, and self-control. The enemy is going to bring people along to distract you from healthy growth in your marriage and to speak hopelessness into it, so you have to have control over who you listen to. Let them know that you have made up your mind to do everything God has been speaking to you about, and you are not going to be confined to anything that would limit the potential of your relationship.

Having self-control is a beneficial resource your mar- riage needs as it goes through a developmental process, and you will see it build over time. Only immature people want to settle for dangling on the edge of barely getting by and letting their emotions rule their words and actions. Keep what God has revealed to you safe, and understand that the relationship you have with the world should not be your story. Apply wisdom to your thoughts and desire a discerning spirit that stays in sync with God and oversees your actions. Only allow patience and self-control as your reactions, as this makes your marriage better. "Live self-controlled, upright and godly lives in this present age"

(Titus 2:12). "[Add] to knowledge, self-control; and to self-control, perseverance" (2 Peter 1:6).

THE PERSEVERANCE OF JESUS

Put forth every effort into growing your character be- cause of the faith you have in God, who established your marriage. "Let us hold unswervingly to the hope we profess, for he who promised is faithful" (Hebrews 10:23). Discipline yourself to keep going, doing everything you can do, and watch your marriage develop over time. "[Love] always protects, always trusts, always hopes, always perseveres" (1 Corinthians 13:7).

Challenge yourself in different ways and be willing to learn through whatever God sends you. Every challenge serves a purpose, so be like a sponge soaking up wisdom that can aid your marriage. You cannot afford to get stuck in a rut based on a temporary situation. Move forward. Have confidence in what your relationship can become, and be satisfied with the time it takes to grow and learn new ways to love your spouse. Find ways to encour- age yourself when marriage feels hard. Look back and see how far you've come. You are not an individual unwilling to learn from your past. Look forward, trusting God's promises. "Imitate those who through faith and patience inherit what has been promised" (Hebrews 6:12).

You are someone not of this world. "Fixing our eyes on Jesus, the pioneer and perfecter of faith. For the joy set before him he endured the cross, scorning its shame, and sat down at the right hand of the throne of God" (Hebrews 12:2, emphasis mine). You and your spouse deserve the best of heaven because Jesus died to give it to you. Believe that good things will come to your marriage because marriage is a gift of God. God wants to bless you, help you, strengthen you, and grow you, so every time you decide to grow in a new way, recognize that the thought is from God and accept the assignment. God sends these thoughts for the purpose of pushing your relationship forward. This information is like a pair of jumper cables you need to jump-start a dead or dying mindset. "Consider him who endured such opposition from sinners, so that you will not grow weary and lose heart" (v. 3).

Stinking thinking is like a dead battery—dead because it filled up with thoughts exclusively about the things that benefited itself. Think about your relationship with God first, receive everything He has to give you and do everything He tells you to, and His spiritual charge will reignite your relationship. The spirit of God will connect with a seed deep inside you and fire you up to win in marriage. You will become a relentless person, because everything you choose to do for your marriage will be because you understand that being like Jesus is for God's pleasure, and His presence and love in your life will overflow to your spouse.

God will subdue your mind to where you are not concerned with what you are going to receive from what you invest in your marriage. God is the one who controls your marital stock market. God is the one who remains calm when things look bad; He knows you will always go through peaks and valleys together. What you invest at the beginning of the process cannot compare to what you will receive at the end of the process. Be a person who is not willing to quit until you see something happen.

There is a debate going around pertaining to the best basketball player ever to play the game. Michael Jordan, Lebron James, and Kareem Abdul-Jabbar are arguably in the top five when it comes to identifying who is the GOAT (greatest of all time). Regardless of where you place these individuals on your list, each one of them possessed the determination to put in the work for the purpose of being the best. They made a wise decision to reject instant gratification for the purpose of playing a game that they are devoted to long term. Their ability to know what they wanted to accomplish allowed them to destroy any obstacle that might interfere with their goals. They successfully eliminated any excuse as to why they could not be the best in the business.

Being the best you can be in your marriage requires that you devote yourself to your marriage by maintain- ing some form of self-discipline. How you conduct yourself is an indicator to your spouse of how serious you are about improving things. The five key components of self-discipline are:

- balance
- calmness
- determination
- confidence
- willpower

God gives you the ability to be sober-minded in your conduct and not quick to act in anger or to make an impulsive decision. Do you want Him to equip you to run a marathon or a sprint? If you choose the sprint, you'll end up being disappointed because marriage is a marathon that requires years of training if you want to win. If you go in thinking it won't take work, you'll probably end up regretting making the decision of saying I do because you'll start lazy and end up with little. "Whatever you do, work at it with all your heart, as working for the Lord" (Colossians 3:23).

GOD'S GRACE IS ENOUGH

Be led by the Spirit. "Those who are led by the Spirit of God are the children of God" (Romans 8:14). He communicates with you and encourages you to do your best to make the marriage better (with grace). Operating in grace empowers your marriage. It causes you to rethink how you view your marriage, and you learn how to appreciate what you have. Having God's grace throughout your marriage helps you function under a protective umbrella that shields your relationship from those things on a mission to destroy it and take it down.

I encourage you to confess out of your mouth and believe in your heart that your marriage is sufficiently built in God and that you have full access to His power, which will strengthen you in times of weakness. You possess heavenly authority given to you to boost your inner man. Once you start using it, people will start asking you what's gotten into you, and you will be able to reveal that God has transformed your mind so radically you now view your marriage with hope. You understand God has given you everything you need for your marriage to be successful.

People are more apt to listen to and receive from someone who is excited about expressing the grace they have rather than receiving from someone who complains about what they do not have. A false narrative has been communicated that grass is greener on the other side of the mountain. It may look greener, but once you do your investigation and see it up close and personal, you will realize that what you saw from the distance is anything but real. Where you currently stand is where you can implement a change that produces a positive effect, thanks to the grace God provides.

To be able to provide the right kind of service to your king or queen, you need to take possession of the authority that's connected to grace. Allow God to be in charge. God has provided you with more than enough grace for your marriage. I beseech you, don't take your marriage and the grace that's upon it for granted. An unpleasant odor reaches God the moment you believe that not enough grace has been provided. The relationship be- tween you and God is what will make your marriage healthy. "He jealously longs for the spirit he has caused to dwell in us. But he gives us more grace. That is why Scripture says: 'God opposes the proud but shows favor to the humble'" (James 4:5–6). A humble person undertakes what's needed for the purpose of being an effective leader—His grace.

In Luke 8:43–48, we read about the woman who had an issue with bleeding. She spoke with and spent a lot of money on several doctors who provided her with different thoughts and ideas on how to deal with her issue, but none of their advice healed her. I believe that she placed her trust in the information, but it wasn't enough. I can see her having less and less faith in believing that the doctors could help. Then, she took the right step in the process of her monumental story. The woman heard about someone by the name of Jesus who had a history of being able to address issues. She made up her mind that this man was someone she could receive help from. The life-changing event took place upon her taking her first step toward Him, extending her arm, and having the faith to be made whole. She believed that she was in the right place at the right time and that her faith was in the right thing. Jesus confirmed this when He said it was her faith that made her new again. "He said to her, 'Daughter, your faith [your personal trust and confidence in Me] has made you well. Go in peace (untroubled, undisturbed well-being)'" (Luke 8:48 AMP).

Have a heart and mind to receive from God, not man, to make you whole. Your marriage is not built on what mankind may say to you; it's what the Word of God confirms in you that matters. Be someone humble enough to know what's needed— more of Jesus. This woman's heal- ing took place when she humbled herself and extended her faith. Your marriage should reflect this kind of faith. Place yourself under the garment of grace. Hum- ble yourself and accept that you do not have the answers on how to function within the confines of a marriage, but God does. Trusting in and acting on the Word of God is the answer to this question.

[And He did this] to fully equip and perfect the saints (God's people) for works of service, to build up the body of Christ [the church]; until we all reach oneness in the faith and in the knowledge of the Son of God, [growing spiritually] to become a mature believer, reaching to the measure of the fullness of Christ [manifesting His spiritual completeness and exercising our spiritual gifts in unity]. So that we are no longer children [spiritually imma- ture], tossed back and forth [like ships on a stormy sea] ... But speaking the truth in love [in all things—both our speech and our lives expressing His truth], let us grow up in all things into Him [fol- lowing His example] who is the Head—Christ.

— – EPHESIANS 4:12–15 (AMP)

CHAPTER 6

Your Shared Vision

Plans to give you hope and a future.
– Jeremiah 29:11

VISION, noun

1. Especially, that which is seen otherwise than by the ordinary sight, or the rational eye; a supernatural, prophetic, ... as, the visions of Isaiah.

– Webster's Dictionary 1913[1]

Birthdays, Mother's Day, Father's Day, and Christmas are days we are excited about based on the expectations we have for them, just like the expectations we have for our marriage. I have witnessed couples with no type of expectation or vision for where they would like to see their marriage end up.

> Write down the revelation and make it plain on tablets so that [he/she] may run with it.
>
> — – HABAKKUK 2:2

Writing down your vision for your marriage is the fuel that your marriage needs. It shows where God is leading your marriage based on what has been revealed to you and what has been received in your heart, and having it helps you run and not walk toward it. Having a God-given vision prevents you from being distracted by the things around you.

You have been given an endorsement from God to see your marriage all the way to the end. A marriage that's connected to a vision cannot fail. It's when we take our eyes off the vision God has placed in our lives that we sway to the left or to the right and don't stay on the straight and narrow path, which is wide enough for those who are obedient.

Every day, when you wake up, you and your spouse should be able to see the vision you have written for your family. This is a reminder to you both of the commitment you have to one another and, more importantly, to God. It reminds you that you agreed to speak and hear the same thing over your marriage.

VISION AND GOALS

Because of the Holy Spirit in you, you have access to the creativity of our heavenly Father to come up with ways of growing your relationship. This is why I believe that being best friends with your spouse is critical for a positive future. A wise spouse understands that they are not married to a perfect person. They take one step at a time toward improvement, maintaining a positive perspective of what potentially could take place. Naturally, you will face some challenges in your relationship, but do not spend your time focusing on what your relationship is not; spend your energy on being a representative of God. Activate your vision—start making it happen. Do not push your agenda for the purpose of getting your way. This way of thinking can isolate your spouse. Build your thoughts on the things above: "Since then, you have been raised with Christ, set your hearts on things above, where Christ is, seated at the right hand of God. Set your mind on things above, not on earthly things. For you died, and your life is now hidden with Christ in God" (Colossians 3:1–3). Let your oneness with Christ impart blessing upon your life and marriage. Present yourself to your spouse as a person who believes in a successful future with them.

Trust and believe that your spouse has your back and is excited about assisting you through the process. God has provided you both with spiritual eyes that allow you to see the impact of every bad decision, not because He desires to see you fail but because you both have the ability to look at your situation from different angles, especially when you deal with pain together.

Stay humble. For Peter to get to the next level, he had to be able to receive harsh correction from Jesus without getting caught up in his feelings. Your marriage was created to be a blessing, and you contain the ability to produce everything you have been believing in God for. Just like Campbell's Soup, your marriage was created to be "M'm! M'm! Good!" based on the ingredients within it.

Make a choice today that you are going to think about your dreams and work on incorporating them in your marriage. But before you move forward, talk with your spouse about your dreams. Listen to what they have to say about it, and decide how to work it into your marriage together.

UNDERSTAND THE VISION

Understanding marriage is vital to understanding the purpose of your marriage. Marriage isn't a to-do list where you score points, and you're a failure if you can't meet all your expectations at once. It's about obtaining a deeper understanding of your spouse and where you flow as one in Christ. It's about taking it one day at a time, letting God develop you as you plan the future. As a wise person, decide that every day, you are going to learn something good you can add to your marriage. Successful people are persistent in receiving knowledge and adding it to their roadmap so their journey can be the best one possible.

"Trust in the Lord with all your heart and lean not on your own understanding; in all your ways submit to him, and he will make your paths straight" (Proverbs 3:5–6). This passage of Scripture does not say that you should seek understanding; it says you should not seek your own understanding. If you only listen to yourself, you'll end up with a god complex and only function from your own knowledge bank, but you can't find true wisdom there. God wants you to be humble enough to seek His understanding so you can have the best relationship possible with your spouse. Will you allow God's gift of understanding to mold the way that you think about your marriage? Will you let His vision and goals be your vision and goals?

Your marriage is a relationship that's created by God for His will and His purposes to come to pass. Your spouse should be just as obsessed with winning in your marriage as you are, and your joint vision should be one that your heavenly Father is excited about.

When Jesus was in the flesh and dwelled on the earth, He did everything with the purpose of receiving approval from His heavenly Father. Even though His flesh desired for Him not to go to the cross, His commitment to doing the will of His Father superseded His desire.

> [Jesus] fell with his face to the ground and prayed, "My Father, if it is possible, may this cup be taken from me. Yet not as I will, but as you will." ... He went away a second time and prayed, "My Father, if it is not possible for this cup to be taken away unless I drink it, may your will be done."
>
> — – MATTHEW 26:39, 42

Just like Jesus, you must trust the spirit of God to give you His vision and to help you understand it. Once He helps you understand the vision and goals, you'll have peace of mind about moving forward. Put forth a concentrated effort in listening to the Holy Spirit and aligning your inner self with His truth. Line up internally with the vision that God has for your relationship.

Your marriage should be built upon a purpose, and it should be for your joint benefit. In a healthy marriage, sides aren't being created where it is being built against you. Your marriage was created by God, and He provided blocks of instruction that are connected to His authority—He possesses the power to deal with any situation.

COMMANDMENTS

Within your vision, there should be a list of commandments that you confess and believe God for. These contain power, and you can regularly confess over yourselves the authority that's designed to hold your marriage together. When reading your commandments, you trust and believe they are action words that require you to do something. A commandment that doesn't require you to do anything is not a commandment. It should require you to put forth maximum effort.

A commandment is written because there is a desire to receive some form of benefit out of it. In trusting God to be involved and at the center of your marriage, you should put down the best things you can think of that will cause your marriage to excel. When you finish writing down what you are believing God for, I believe that He looks at your list and says, "Is that it?" The beautiful thing about God is that He always holds up His end of the bargain—His promises are true.

Your marriage commitment is based on the relationship built between you and God. It is vital to your marriage that you build it on the love that was first established between you and God. If you don't have a solid foundation, you will not have faith in the promise of a relationship that will bring your dreams to pass. When we are committed and full of faith that God will come through, He shows Himself to be strong and honorable to His Word. Pursue things that are honorable. They contain value, and the pursuit of them is a rewarding process that builds your relationship up. God is at the apex of the relationship, and He created you with the ability to go through a process and grow in it. Having an understanding that your work in not in vain should encourage you, and possessing a clear vision for where you are heading will keep you on the right path.

Having a list attached to your vision is a beautiful thing, because every time you see things accomplished, it builds up your faith. An unspeakable joy comes over you, and the faith you have in your marriage expands. This joy, the inner work of the Holy Spirit, starts inside you and then overflows to affect things around you. You change from the inside out rather than people changing you from the outside in.

Writing down your commandments is vital. It reminds you that the mission of the family is priority number one. In coming together to write your commandments, you are working together to stay healthy no matter what comes up. Your commandments are reminders to keep outside influences out of your marriage.

I recommend that one of the commandments you have in your marriage statement is that you will always speak the truth in love. "Speaking the truth in love, we will grow to become in every respect the mature body of him who is the head, that is, Christ. From him the whole body joined and held together by every supporting ligament, grows and builds itself up in love" (Ephesians 4:15–16). The way that you communicate with your words is essential to your development. Speaking in truth and love is the key to opening doors to an endless number of opportunities. Christ conducted Himself under the authority of truth and love and communicated in love and truth. As His representative, you should communicate with your spouse the way Jesus would. This doesn't mean that what you say is always going to feel good, nor does it mean that what your spouse says to you will, but when you have a mature attitude, you will accept that what is being communicated is designed to help you and not hurt you.

> Jesus sometimes seemed a little harsh. At one point He was speaking to Peter, and Peter had a God-like kind of vision:
>
> "What about you?" [Jesus] asked. "Who do you say I am?"
>
> Simon Peter answered, "You are the Messiah, the Son of the living God."
>
> Jesus replied, "Blessed are you, Simon son of Jonah, for this was not revealed to you by flesh and blood, but by my Father in heaven."
>
> — – MATTHEW 16:15–17

Yet, just a few minutes after this personal encounter with God, Peter lost his focus and stopped seeing things God's way because of his fear. He opened his mouth and spoke outside of spiritual alignment:

Jesus began to explain to his disciples that he must go to Jerusalem and suffer many things at the hands of the elders, the chief priests and the teachers of the law, and that he must be killed and on the third day be raised to life.

Peter took him aside and began to rebuke him. "Never, Lord!" he said. "This shall never happen to you!"

Jesus turned and said to Peter, "Get behind me, Satan! You are a stumbling block to me; you do not have in mind the concerns of God, but merely human concerns."

— – MATTHEW 16:21–23

Jesus recognized that Peter was no longer in tune with God's voice. He had just shared His life purpose, and Peter tried to tell Him He was wrong! Jesus knew who was really talking and fixed it. Can you imagine Pe- ter's facial expression after just being called blessed be- cause of receiving revelation from the spirit of God to being corrected because of speaking from a place of fear (spirit of the Devil) by the same God that he served? Im- agine if Peter hadn't been mature enough to handle what had been spoken to him. Instead, Peter proved his maturity by receiving the word of God that was out to change his life. Speaking in love or being on its receiv- ing end is not going to always make you feel good. Jesus said what He said to Peter because He knew His purpose was more important than Peter's feelings. Additionally, He understood that what He was doing was ultimately going to be beneficial for Peter.

PLANT GOOD SEEDS

Throughout the world, farmers have a vision of the crop they expect to receive from the seeds they plant. They find a fertile field that will cause their seeds to grow.

They are not set in their ways based on a disbelief that their vision of a good harvest potentially could not come to pass. They are motivated and willing to break up the fallow ground and plant. It's the same with having a vision of the marriage you want. You have to know without a shadow of a doubt that your seeds of faith have been planted in the fallow ground of your marriage so it can grow. These seeds are from the Creator. He knows what it takes to get the seed to produce a great crop, and He promises to bless it as it grows.

> I give you every seed-bearing plant on the face of the whole earth and every tree that has fruit with seed in it.
>
> — – GENESIS 1:29

> All these blessings will come on you and accompany you if you obey the Lord your God: ... The fruit of your

womb will be blessed, and the crops of your land. ... The Lord your God will bless you in the land he is giving you. ... The Lord will grant you abundant prosperity—in ... the crops of your ground—in the land he swore to your ancestors to give you.

— – DEUTERONOMY 28:2, 4, 8, 11

Productivity is possible based on the correct resources being used. We choose our resources based on the creativity of our vision and the seeds planted. In structuring your marriage, it's what you surround the seed with that causes it to produce. There are so many things a seed needs to produce, like fertilizer, which is added to the soil or land to increase fertility. Not all fertilizer is the same. Some fertilizers are plant-based and break down quickly, while others, like alfalfa, add drainage and moisture retention to poor soils. Some take watering and a few days to release their nutrients before the farmer begins to see their results. These fertilizing agents have different functions, but they serve the same purpose. It's up to the farmer to apply the right fertilizer to produce the results they are looking for.

The resources you surround your marriage with are vital to the success of your marriage. To have two people coming together to function and operate in oneness, you must provide the perfect mix of warmth, refreshment, nutrients, safety, and love, and all these only come from God. Look at your marriage from His perspective to make it special, and ask Him how to grow it His way. Learn how to appreciate what you have and apply the correct type of fertilizer around your marriage so the fruit that evolves from the seed is strong.

The seeds, or vows, in your marriage, were created by God, and He has mandated them to produce. The vows that were spoken when you stood before God are the perfect seeds, but they must grow. God constructed marriages. He knows what it is going to take for you to remain together "until death do you part." He will provide everything needed to get there.

> God said, "Let the land produce vegetation: seed-bearing plants and trees on the land that bear fruit with seed in it, according to their various kinds." And it was so. The land produced vegetation: plants bearing seed according to their kinds and trees bearing fruit with seed in it according to their kinds. And God saw that it was good.
>
> — – GENESIS 1:11–12

God's words are so powerful. If His words are powerful enough to create the world, open your mind to what they can do to your marriage. Imagine if God had not opened His mouth and spoken this world in existence!

He created seed-bearing plants and trees because He knew what was needed. Your marriage is created to be a promise-keeping, seed-producing, manifestation-producing relationship. You have been given the ability to ensure that you have victory in your marriage based on your obedience to the Word. Being obedient shows that you are mature enough to handle the responsibilities that come with being with your spouse. As a Father who's aware of who you are, He will handpick every resource He gives you for the purpose of growing your relationship. Grow with Him. Grow with your spouse. Keep moving your relationship forward. Place a high value in knowing that your marriage is not a mistake. The vows/seeds within your marriage should not be wasted but treasured. Every seed that comes from a healthy place has a purpose and plan. God knows what He is do- ing with you both.

MAKE THIS SHIP SAIL

It's the spirit of God that guides your relationship (SHIP—it's designed to carry things). Understand your responsibility and authority to direct your ship. You have a heavenly Captain, and He has made you responsible for everything that takes place on the ship. You get to okay who or what has access to your ship, just as you are responsible for what you allow to take place in your relationship. Just like Jesus addressed Peter, you get to address situations in prayer and let the Devil know he is not authorized to be in your relationship. The only reason why people have issues is because they are afraid to speak of change. Negativity is one key that gives access to your ship, but speaking life is the security guard that stops it. I embolden you to be on guard at all times to stop fear, shame, hopelessness, and negativity from destroying your earthen vessel.

The earthen vessel (relationship) that you are in belongs to the one who created it. God is always greater than problems in your marriage. "There is one body and one Spirit, just as you were called to one hope when you were called; one Lord, one faith, one baptism; one God and Father of all, who is over all and through all and in all" (Ephesians 4:4–6). He has all the solutions.

Just like there are items required to create a good stock for a stew, so are there items needed to develop your relationship. Your work is not in vain. What has been invested is beneficial. The best stock is one that marinates over time. The ingredients fuse together to create a unique flavor and fill you up. Your satisfaction in your relationship will directly reflect how much goodness you have invested in the stock. God is genuinely interested in seeing your marriage marinate over the years.

Marinating means you are trusting God in the process, not stressing over feeling like you must be in charge of everything. Allow God to be in charge. Relax while granting Him access to your inner man. He will drop in the appropriate ingredients to allow you to marinate and produce a good stock, adding flavor to your marriage rather than stripping it of flavor. To be great at anything you do, you have to make your heart available to change. You have to let Him in.

Steer your relationship on the right route. Take on board the supplies needed to ensure you make it to your destination—the vision you have decided to write out together. Proper preparation will affect how much you enjoy your trip. Enjoy the journey.

God the Father knows rocky seas are going to come, but He also knows how to speak to the rough seas and command them to be still, and the wind and waves obey. God understands the reasons behind the storm and speaks peace to the source. When things get rocky, aim to learn the real reasons behind the storms so you can speak peace to them. Peace will empower your relationship and keep it on course.

What's in the relationship not only empowers it but it also protects it from getting destroyed by the adversary. A sound goes off when danger comes near, threatening the goal of your marriage: to be a reflection of the type of relationship Jesus and God have.

> I pray ... that all of them may be one, Father, just as you are in me and I am in you. May they also be in us ... I have given them the glory that you gave me, that they may be one as we are one—I in them and you in me—so that they may be brought to complete unity.
>
> — – JOHN 17:20–23

You are husband and wife on this earth to show others you are on the same sheet of music. Two are becoming one, willing to work together with the Spirit of God within you to ensure the rhythm is right. Work together to be able to dwell together as one unit. Move together in agreement and be like Jesus so you can raise the standard of love high in your marriage. Love will cause your spouse to want to hear you and trust you, and trust the journey God has you both on. Trusting the process creates hope and builds your faith in your joint ability to build a strong marriage.

Know that you are more than a conqueror when you are in sync with your Father. Investing what He gives into the marriage comes with the promise of fulfilled desires. "Hope deferred makes the heart sick, but a longing fulfilled is a tree of life" (Proverbs 13:12). Your marriage does not give you what you want; it gives you what God loves to give, and God's plans for you are always good.

The Word of God is here to teach you how to be like Jesus. Be an extraordinary spouse rather than average. Be an exceptional spouse. Make others so jealous of your strong relationship that they ask you for help. Renew your mind with the Word so that you never veer off course toward divorce. Know what pushes your marriage to the next level. Believe you can turn your marriage into a healthy one.

While on the SHIP, make profitability part of your long-term vision plan. Store items in the hold in preparation for future needs. They will make your transition to the next level easier, and sometimes, you will receive them early so you can see that your marriage is bigger than you. These investments should not be placed within reach of people who do not understand the things you have gone through together. They might become jealous of your marriage, thinking you have it easy with your spouse when it has taken hard work on both your parts to get it to where it is today. Enjoy the trust you share with each other, and keep investing kindness and support in each other.

Learn how to let your guard down with your spouse. You have been equipped with someone who desires to connect with you and build you up. You can grow from just doing the right thing into feeling whole and fulfilled with your spouse. Build from the position of excellence—find pleasure in lifting one another up. Find the courage to avoid the negativity of friends. You don't want those negative seeds in your marriage; they will place you and your spouse at odds. God's desire for you both is to get your marriage to the place where you are intertwined. Find a way to stir up the desire to continue working on growing closer. Only the weak do not want to put forth the energy to fight for what's important.

Every step you take is a step closer to your hope of working together. Working with one another is like a knife and a rock—the more you rub that knife against it, the sharper it becomes. The more you work together on a common goal, the better off you will be.

ADJUSTING THE SAIL

In your marriage, if you can't agree on a decision, God must have the final say. He'll give you everything you need to adjust your inner man to where you can come to a place of agreement. Let His Word be the ultimate standard. The beautiful thing about the Word of God is that God can not only see you both as you are today in the marriage, He can also see you as you will become. His decisions keep that in mind, whereas you cannot see the beginning from the end.

Seeing through God's eyes puts your marriage in its proper context. Live your life according to the way He lived on earth. Striving for this kind of character doesn't mean that you are weak; it means you have a standard about who and whose you are. Seeing your marriage from God's eyes gives you the best information about it, whereas incorrect positioning will cause you to miss out on a certain shot. Having the right information means you can take care of any issue quickly God's way.

Making decisions is like adjusting the thermostat in your house. Before you make it colder, you should be considerate of others by asking them how they believe they will be affected by the adjustment. If you don't do this, gear up for a disagreement that could have been avoided. Make adjustments in your marriage the same way. You might want to start hiking together because you think it will bring you closer together, but your decision-making process needs to be predicated on your spouse's actual desire, not what you assume they want. Start the discussion with the goal of peace, and listen as your spouse talks about how they feel at the thought of hiking every week. Speak from a position of love. You are not the only person affected by the decision. If your spouse is completely against the idea, see if, together, you can come up with another activity you can do together that will give you the closeness you are seeking.

Transforming from an ordinary person to a person who is extra ordinary means you see differently. Ordi- nary people do not appreciate their spouse. They tend to become complacent about the relationship. They forget that the energy it took to get into the marriage is going to take twice as much energy in keeping it growing. Extraordinary people are willing to do the little things to keep their spouse's attention. Having a servant's heart is a prior- ity. Your reward will be bigger than what you have invested because by serving and placing all your focus on what your spouse thinks, wants, and needs, you will gain lifelong understanding that promises smooth sailing days ahead.

Understanding your spouse transforms the way you think about your work on, or investment, in the marriage. This is not something you can do at full speed. It takes consistency. You're on a sailing ship, not a motor- boat. If you are about the business of getting things done, start today, because this can take a while. If you are dragging your feet in your pursuit of happiness, do not get upset over the slow return from your investment. I pray that you move forward with a clear conscience and put 100 percent of your effort into your marriage.

LONG-SUFFERING

Legend has it that Walt Disney was turned down 302 times before finally receiving the financing for his dream creation of Walt Disney World. Colonel Sanders was rejected 1,009 times before finding an investor in his chicken recipe. Albert Einstein did not speak until he was four years of age. Steve Harvey, Jim Carrey, and Eric Thomas were homeless at one point in their lives.

These are examples of people suffering through something that could have destroyed them, but they realized that for greatness to come out of them, they had to keep going. They had a vision of what they were aiming for, and they were patient enough to wait for it to come to pass.

Waiting patiently does not mean that it is going to be easy. You will need to stay focused on your vision and goals. Is your thought worthy? Are you building on something that is valuable?

A vision that comes from God means He considers you valuable enough to want to realize His plans through you. Know the plans that He has for you and your marriage. Understanding them should encourage you to not quit on your marriage. He can give you the strength to look the enemy in the eye and let him know that you are in this marriage for the long haul. When you have this type of mindset, it closes the door to divorce being an option.

> Job replied to the Lord:
> "I know that you can do all things;
> no purpose of yours can be thwarted.
> You asked, 'Who is this that obscures my plans without knowledge?'
> Surely I spoke of things I did not understand,
> things too wonderful for me to know."
>
> — – JOB 42:1–3

You can be excited about investing in your marriage when you have a better understanding about the value of your relationship and how good it could be. Awaken your vision. Take a closer look at what makes you good together and find out what makes it profitable. Invest the time and energy into building your marriage on purpose. You are in your marriage for the long haul, so make it worth your while!

In times of suffering, know that your relationship is protected. The process can be agonizing, but as you go through it, you can make your marriage better purely by receiving all God has to give you during your suffering. A lifelong marriage is obtainable. Couples like my parents will tell you that there was a time or two in their relationship when they thought about quitting, but they focused on what could be instead of what wasn't, arrived at agreement, and came up with a joint plan on how to move forward. When your marriage is built on a solid foundation, you don't give up because it's what holds you up. Keep going. It won't be long before you find yourself in a place where you learn how to celebrate one another again. "The God of all grace, who called you to his eternal glory in Christ, after you have suffered a little while, will himself restore you and make you strong, firm and steadfast. To him be the power forever and ever" (1 Peter 5:10–11).

Straighten your spine and stand up against a hostile mental environment telling you to quit. A mind that's split between two opinions creates a hostile environment in your home. Disciple your conduct. Enter the King's domain and uphold your vows. Spend time in the Word and make sure your desires line up with God's. Think healthy thoughts. Listen to what God is saying so you can see a roadmap to what's next. Ask Him what you might encounter along the way. Read your original marriage vows, vision statement, and marriage goals. Having a roadmap for your marriage early on seals the deal and removes doubts about your expectations. You are no longer wishing upon a star. You are in the business of taking ownership of what's best for you and your spouse. It is worth your time to wait on what will come out of your investment. You are transforming from ordinary to extraordinary.

We know that in all things God works for the good of those who love him, who have been called according to his purpose.

— – ROMANS 8:28

When you are looking for your dream job, you know a few things in advance:

1. You first believe that you possess enough good skills to do the job.
2. You put in an application.
3. You interview.
4. The potential employer makes sure you are who they thought you were, based on your résumé.
5. You get the job.
6. Over time, you show you were either a good or bad choice for the position. If you are who they thought you were, you will assist the company in reaching its goals by making the company stronger.
7. To show their appreciation for what you have accomplished, the company will (should) in return invest into you by providing opportunities for growth—through learning opportunities and a pay raise.
8. If you take the opportunity for granted and don't do your part in living up to your agreement, your supervisor will find a way to get rid of you.

Within your marriage, it is not wise to take on the type of mentality displayed in number 8. Remain peaceful, and allow the spirit of God within to affect your attitude. Think through the process required for number 6. Listen, learn, work hard, support your spouse, grow. All these actions prepare you for your destiny. The end goal is to allow God's grace to overcome you until you display the character of Jesus.

GOODNESS

Whatever comes against you cannot stop you because of the goodness of God. Your faith is built on this foundation. Your wisdom comes from Him. "Surely your goodness and love will follow me all the days of my life, and I will dwell in the house of the Lord forever" (Psalm 23:6). God filled you with His goodness and love for your spouse, and goodness desires to follow you for the rest of your life. Agreeing with this thought will have you dwelling in the house of God forever, which will also make your relationship profitable. Work on possessing the power of the goodness of God.

Goodness means you provide aid to the areas where your spouse has been wounded. Set a precedent for how much respect you have for your relationship and your willingness to lead in love, so much so that your spouse wants to love in the same way. Be willing to do whatever it takes to push away the cares of the world and the issues of life so they don't distract you from walking in goodness in your marriage. Follow Him, and be excited about the relationship you have. Acknowledge His greatness and allow it to fill your marriage so it will not fail.

Don't let anything destroy the dreams you have for your marriage. Do not give up, do not give in, and continue to walk out your journey. Following through on your vows is attractive to the eyes and nurturing to the spirit. Your relationship will continue to move forward based on the momentum generated by God's goodness on your wedding day.

FAITH

Family, be satisfied in your marriage, and rejoice be- cause God has built your confidence in believing that you have received the best He can offer, even in uncomfortable times. He is a promise keeper, and He does not hold back the things that are needed for your marriage to grow. He puts things in place to ensure that your promises come to pass. God's Word for your marriage is more important than anything anyone else has ever said about it or ever will. Your future is bright because you have a clear vision for your marriage. Having it is like looking in the face of God every day. He will bring your desires to pass.

Expect only God's best to come out of what you have invested in. Planting God-given seeds in your marriage can only produce a good harvest for your family. As the planter, do your part by ensuring that it's fully protected so it can grow up and produce pure fruit. "Once more, a remnant of the kingdom of Judah will take root below and bear fruit above" (Isaiah 37:31).

Your faith for your marriage must have deep roots to prevent the cares of this world from destroying your trust in His promises. Your seed for your marriage will generate and produce. I cannot say it enough: Your marriage will come forth and it will produce, and the harvest you'll see will be because of your hard work nurturing it.

The size of a tree above ground reflects how deep the roots of the tree go below the ground. Just like a tree, the roots of the Word of God will cause your marriage to develop and show the world what's possible.

> Joseph named his firstborn Manasseh and said, "It is because God has made me forget all my trouble and all my father's household." The second son he named Ephraim and said, "It is because God has made me fruitful in the land of my suffering."
>
> — – GENESIS 41:51–52

You have been justified by God to produce a harvest that's fruitful for your marriage. "Those he called, he also justified; those he justified, he also glorified" (Romans 8:30). Good fruit starts growing from the inside out and not from the outside in. Learn how to speak to your marriage from the position of being able to see the outcome before it takes place. Every day you can wake up knowing that your marriage can only improve and get better. Declare:

- My marriage cannot fail.

- My marriage can only produce things that are beneficial for it.

There are benefits connected to speaking words of affirmation over your marriage and operating your life in a way that makes your Father well pleased. Show the world through your marriage that the Word of God is true and that everything must be obedient to His Word to be productive.

The fragrance of marriage to the one you love is attractive to your inner senses. Your spouse should be the only fragrance that you desire to put on. If you desire a different fragrance, you're being misled about what's attractive to you. The only fragrance that God places on your relationship is the one He planted there, and He gave you the gift of being drawn to it—not for what you could get out of it but because of what you could give. You have been given the grace to run after God's resources for your marriage to *your* spouse.

The grace of God is significant enough to carry your relationship where you are weak. Your efforts might look good to you but not to God, when you account for what has been invested in you. There's probably so much more you could invest. Build your spiritual muscles by reading and applying the Word of God to your relationship. It is just like Prego Spaghetti Sauce: "It's in there!"

Have faith. Keep a winning attitude. A relationship that lacks success is one that has two parties who refuse to have a conversation with the one who created it. Talk with your spouse about your marriage truthfully. Make sure your spouse feels heard, just as the Lord hears you. "The Lord is near to all who call on him, to all who call on him in truth. He fulfills the desires of those who fear him; he hears their cry and saves them. The Lord watches over all who love him" (Psalm 145:18–20).

God is at the center of your marriage. He is listening in on your conversations. He is nothing like mankind, where you wonder if He is going to be able to come through. Operate on a one-step-at-a-time mentality, and keep asking Him questions so you can plan your growth. God the Father operates outside of time. He goes against the grain and is able to do what He said He would do. This is why you have to keep Him as the cen- terpiece of your relationship. The more you build your faith, the more you will start to believe that "It's in there!"

OUR MARRIAGE VISION

CHIEF GOAL

We will encourage people to believe that in God's eyes, they are special and that God created them with value.

DECLARATIONS FOR OUR MARRIAGE

1. We have faith that God has implanted the right kind of stuff in us to help our marriage grow, and that He is the open door to a healthy marriage.
2. We understand that growing our marriage does not mean that every day is going to be a day we enjoy.

3. We believe God has equipped us with the tools we need to walk through difficult times together.
4. We are thankful for our marriage.
5. We believe God created our marriage to flow with milk and honey.

PERSONAL GOALS FOR OUR MARRIAGE

1. We will be wise in making decisions together with the goal of peaceful agreements.
2. We will allow the spirt of God to assist us in working on our issues in order to become whole.
3. We believe that the way we think about our marriage affects the way we conduct ourselves, so we will always see it as a gift from God.
4. We will love each other like Christ loves us.
5. We will respect each other's unique perspective on everything, no matter how we feel about it.

*Faith is the substance of things hoped for,
the evidence of things not seen.*
– Hebrews 11:1

CHAPTER 7

Fight for Your Marriage

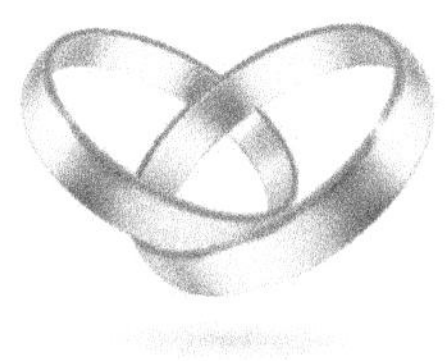

Take your stand against the devil's schemes.
– Ephesians 6:10

FIGHT, verb

1. To strive or contend for victory, with armies or in single combat; to attempt to defeat, subdue, or destroy an enemy, ...

2. To act in opposition to anything; to struggle against; to contend; to strive; to make resistance. ...

To fight it out, to fight until a decisive and conclusive result is reached.

– Webster's Dictionary 1913[1]

The true goal of the enemy is to build a barrier between you and God. He can accomplish this if you stop making your marriage and your relationship with God a priority. The enemy will also do all he can to create barriers between you both to make your relationship difficult, but he can't unless he has access to it. He wants to build this barrier up so high between you that you think it's impossible to move forward.

> Be strong in the Lord and in his mighty power. Put on the full armor of God, so that you can take your stand against the devil's schemes. For our struggle is not against flesh and blood, but against the rulers, against the authorities, against the powers of this dark world and against the spiritual forces of evil in the heavenly realms. Therefore, put on the full armor of God so that when the day of evil comes, you may be able to stand your ground, and after you have done everything, to stand.
>
> Stand firm then, with the belt of truth buckled around your waist, with the breastplate of righteousness in place, and with your feet fitted with the readiness that comes from the gospel of peace. In addition to all this, take up the shield of faith, with which you can extinguish all the flaming. arrows of the evil one. Take the helmet of salvation and the sword of the Spirit, which is the word of God. And pray in the Spirit on all occasions with all kinds of prayers and requests. With this in mind, be alert.
>
> — – EPHESIANS 6:10–18, EMPHASES MINE

The armor of God will protect you from the enemy's devices, protecting your mind, your determination to fight, your willingness to stay vulnerable, and your desire to walk with God.

Keep hoping and expecting that something good is going to enter into your marriage so you can stay ener- gized enough to fight for the things you believe in. Ask your spouse to fight with you instead of fighting against you so your shared vision from God remains the same. If not, your spouse's vision will change to a pathway on how to escape the relationship. Fight for your marriage like Jacob fought God for a blessing:

> Jacob was left alone, and a Man [came and] wrestled with him until daybreak. When the Man saw that He had not prevailed against Jacob, He touched his hip joint; and Jacob's hip was dislocated as he wrestled with Him. Then He said, "Let Me go, for day is breaking." But Jacob said, "I will not let You go unless You declare a blessing on me." ... And He declared a blessing [of the covenant promises] on Jacob there.
>
> — – GENESIS 32:24–26, 29 (AMP)

Jacob was so focused in getting what his heart de- sired that God had to dislocate his hip to break free from his grasp. Jacob was in great pain, but he still held on for the blessing. Like Jacob, don't give up, and be will- ing to fight for a blessed marriage.

SEE WHAT'S POSSIBLE WITH GOD

The fight for your marriage starts in your mind. Everything about you was created in a unique and special way, including the way you think. God feeds your mind with a better understanding about who you are and how you can make your dreams reality. Your dream that you have about your marriage can be bigger than the fear of failing within it. Be bold enough to fantasize about what you can have. It will encourage you to come up with a productive plan that leads to the pleasures of a happy marriage. Put in the work and reject any doubts that will cloud your vision. Some people say your marriage is what you see. I say that your marriage is what you know it could be, what you make it, and what you do to protect it.

The faith that you have for your relationship did not come from you; it came from the same source as the grace for your marriage—God the Father. Place your eyes on what has been given to you, the gift above all gifts, a guide map that will turn your relationship right side up again: your relationship with God.

Hold the vision high. The physical effort that's put into your marriage isn't the most important thing; your willingness to let God guide your thoughts is what's important. An immature spouse is full of pride and lacks humility, ill-equipped to do what's needed for the improvement of the relationship and unwilling to seek wisdom. A tempered person seeks help for the purpose of making their God-given dreams come to pass. See what's possible with God and act on it. "We make it our goal to

please him, whether we are at home in the body or away from it"
(2 Corinthians 5:9).

Your marriage was created to fulfill the Father's purpose.
Knowing Him means knowing how to hold your marriage
together. You don't have to do everything to find joy in your
marriage because God is always at work. His Word connects with
you and gives you rest, building up your faith in His promises to
trust that He's in control of each situation, of your conduct, and
of your marriage. He is gentle with you as you work toward the
vision, and you can be gentle with your spouse. Let His love win
you both over.

God created the institution of marriage with the resources
necessary to sustain you and keep you excited about being with
your spouse. God, being a spirit, is alive in your marriage, and He
desires that you and your spouse have faith in being able to move
together as one unit to attain your goals.

Faith is the assurance (title deed, confirmation) of things
hoped for (divinely guaranteed) and the evidence of
things not seen [the conviction of their reality—faith
comprehends as fact what cannot be experienced by the
physical senses]. For by this [kind of] faith, the men of old
gained [divine] approval. By faith [that is, with an
inherent trust and enduring confidence in the power,
wisdom and goodness of God], we understand ... that
what is seen was not made out of things which are visible.

— – HEBREWS 11:1–3 (AMP)

This Scripture provides you with enough strength to trust that your marriage will make it. God's perspective of your marriage comes with expectations. He wants you to see it the way He does so you can get on board with the way He plans on manifesting the seeds of your vision. The Creator understands the type of outcome that's needed. Do not allow the pressures of life to ruin what can potentially take place based on what you are afraid to place your hope in.

The faith that you have in your marriage is the driving force behind speaking a blessed marriage into existence. The more good things you speak about your marriage, the more you are going to see the manifestation take place in your relationship. God has blessed you with hope and faith to gain tangible, obtainable things. Knowing that you can obtain them means there is no way you are going to fail in your efforts.

Denzel Washington is viewed as one of the best actors in the business because he always had faith in his vision of being the best. Believe that you have the best spouse in the world, and you give them room to become the best. Faith is never wasted; it feeds a marriage. Hope is never a mistake because it's placed in God.

God has given you the assurance to know that as long as you believe in Him, your marriage will last for the duration. The day you said your vows before God and to your spouse, God recorded them, and they resonated with you. There was a twinkling in your heart as you said the words, believing that your spouse would always love you, treat you with respect, be there for you, and see you in the light that God created you in—and you promised you would do the same. Seal the deal on your marriage by developing the relationship with your spouse to where it could potentially go.

Everything you need is within your relationship and is God-given. Dig deep. Find out what it's capable of doing. Mighty men and women of God, at some point, found their faith being put to the test, and during those times, they had to dig into God and not give up so they could honor their commitment. Just like they were put to the test, your marriage is going to be put to the test. When you find yourself in a difficult situation where you feel powerless, you are going to have to remember the purpose of your marriage if you want a testimony. Make sure your commitment to one another is not moved by the things you see. Trust that everything God revealed about your marriage will come to pass. The gift of the Holy Spirit is designed to lead and direct your relationship into all truth so that your vows will be fulfilled.

AUTHORITY OVER YOUR THOUGHTS

Think about what the future can bring: If you're struggling in your marriage right now, looking at it in its current state through your own eyes only makes it worse. Only by letting the Spirit transform your mind and by seeing what it can become grows it into what it can be.

God is present right now: Your heart lives in a place of joy with Him already. Doing life with Him is a wonderful way to live. Likewise, when you choose to be with someone for life, God promises that your marriage can be a place where you find joy, too —His joy. His presence brings joy that can change a situation because you make choices based on hope and trust. Trust that your Father wants your marriage full of His love, and He will provide His full support as you walk with Him in it. Connect mentally with what your marriage will become. Once you can do this, you start the habit of trusting what you believe in and hope for.

It is the hope and joy of the Lord within the marriage that causes a change to take place. This does not mean we are not required to do anything, but in knowing the outcome, we move toward what we desire to see happen.

Believe a great marriage is possible: Learn to fall in love with the thought of being in a marriage that gives you a sense of meaning and value. Put forth the energy into living in a place of peace within your relationship. Do not allow anyone to tell you that your marriage was not created to be a blessing. You have one life to live, and the life that you choose to live is an encouragement to others to see that a great marriage is possible.

Falling in love with the Holy Spirit opens your mind and your heart toward the kind of love you can have in your marriage. Know that the Holy Spirit provides you with a different way of thinking about your relationship, and believe that unconditional love can develop.

You are not in your relationship to conform to anyone else's negative ideas of how things will be. The patterns of your thought processes can be changed to God's thought processes. Whatever you deal with is just a test, which you can pass to let others know that a good marriage is possible. It's letting God's

Word renew your mind that will make this level of faith part of your life.

AUTHORITY WITH YOUR WORDS

Your marriage was not created by man; it was established and approved by God. It dwells under the covering of His holy Word. Your marriage was spoken into existence based on the power of the words spoken out of your mouth. Proverbs 21:23 (AMP) says, "He who guards his mouth and his tongue guards himself from troubles." This verse is a clear indication that you should be mindful of the things that flow out of your mouth, including your marriage vows. The relationship you have with your spouse is a reflection of the vows you have spoken. The only reason you spoke to them is because you believed them, as you should believe them today. If you don't, your heart has been corrupted, which will cause you problems—what comes out of your mouth lets you know what's affecting your heart. Learn how to make your mouthpiece work in your favor. Speak what you believe and have faith in. Over time, you will see your marriage start to transition.

We should not allow our flesh to cause us to speak something that does not come from heaven above. When you open your mouth to speak about your marriage, speak what you expect to come to pass. The moment you open your mouth to speak in faith, the heavens respond.

The way that you go about winning the fight for your marriage is by taking a stand for what you believe with your mouth. Take up your shield and be willing to fight for your relationship. Do not get caught up in what your adversary wants you to believe. Do what's required to have a successful marriage. Be persistent in speaking against the powers of darkness. Darkness only possesses the ability to see its potential to destroy, but if your ar- mor is on, you are both protected from its devices. Knowing that you are shielded from the threats of the enemy builds your confidence in what you are capable of doing in prayer.

Put it in your mind that whatever situation you are facing is under your control, and it must be obedient to the words you speak out of your mouth. Stop imagining the worst, and know that the relationship you are in was created to dwell in greatness. "The Lord will make you the head, not the tail. If you pay attention to the commands of the Lord your God that I give you this day and carefully follow them, you will always be at the top, never at the bottom" (Deuteronomy 28:13). Every day when you wake up, say to yourself, "I am going to make my marriage better than it was yesterday."

TAKE RESPONSIBILITY FOR YOUR MARRIAGE

Keeping God at the center of your marriage is a priority, as it affects its potential fruit. Just like your heavenly Father does with you, focus your attention on lifting up your spouse in the natural as well as in the spiritual. Accept every opportunity to amplify your marriage as a gift. It is attractive to walk about the earth with a smile on your face, knowing you are doing something that makes your spouse feel good about being with you.

Be filled with the Holy Spirit (Acts 13:52). This is the will of God—that His children are charged up with His power, sent through the divine connection that we have with Him. When you understand what you have access to, it opens your eyes to what can come to pass. I am here to encourage you to never give up on the potential that's in your marriage. It's like watching your children from the day they are born. As long as they have breath in their body, you continue to see what they potentially can become. That's the spirit of God opening your eyes to future possibilities. Stay hopeful. Don't give up on your destiny together. "[Like a boxer] I strictly discipline my body and make it my slave, so that, after I have preached [the gospel] to others, I myself will not somehow to be disqualified [as unfit for service]" (1 Corinthians 9:27 AMP).

Sanctify your relationship. Practice self-discipline when it comes to natural appetites and passions. God created all our natural senses for us to function in an effective way. Living in this flesh, our senses can tell us we must have certain things, but they lie a lot. They should be trained to obey the truth. You can use your own strength and self-sufficiency to moderate your senses regularly, but with God, you also need to take His daily power shots to stay strong enough to keep saying no to anything that will not bless your marriage. The everlasting energy of His Holy Spirit gives you the strength to power up your relationship. Even though you are in your body, it doesn't have the authority to tell you how to live your life. You have been given the responsibility to take control of everything that takes place in your relationship —good or bad. You choose what stays and grows, and you choose what must stay out. When you stay mentally in sync with God, this becomes easy over time.

KEEP YOUR MARRIAGE ON THE RIGHT CONSTRUCTION PLAN

In December 2017, my wife and I were blessed enough to move into our first home that we purchased together. It took eight months, from the day we signed the paperwork, to build the house. With me working an hour and a half away, only my wife was close enough to the new house to keep an eye on its construction. Throughout that process, she identified issues with the home, so she hired someone who could validate her concerns and then mandated that the issues be corrected. One issue was with the roofing of the house, and thanks to the information she had, she was successful in getting the entire roof replaced. The reason my wife did what she did had nothing to do with the cosmetic appearance of the exterior; it was about the importance of having a house built according to the architect's plans.

The foundation of a house is the principal part of building a house according to plan, and the foundation of your relationship is the same way. It's the most valuable step, accurately calculated and created to withstand the pressure that will be placed on the foundation. Creating a strong foundation for your marriage based on the Word and God's sacrificial love is a process that includes marinating your mind in the Word and using it as the filter for the constant influx of information that comes through.

Truth strengthens your will to do what's right and empowers your marriage.

God is our great encourager, our rock, and our salva- tion. "I trust in your unfailing love; my heart rejoices in your salvation. I will sing the Lord's praise, for he has been good to me" (Psalm 13:5–6). Be the stone that's committed to staying in the relationship, anchored in the Word that's designed to train your mind in all you need:

The Spirit of the Lord will rest on him—
>   the Spirit of wisdom and of understanding,
>   the Spirit of counsel and of might,
>   the Spirit of the knowledge and fear of the Lord—
>   and he will delight in the fear of the Lord.
>   He will not judge by what he sees with his eyes,
>   or decide by what he hears with his ears.

— – ISAIAH 11:2–3

The more you understand what God is doing in your marriage, the more you will find yourself committed to His building plan.

Don't allow outside influences to distract you from your purpose. Don't become limited in hope and faith. Build your marriage based on the goals of the building plan. Keep seeing the bigger picture, and fight to keep the construction going. Set up alarm systems to provide warning signs when things that do not belong in your marriage get too close. A lot of time and energy has been invested in your marriage. Don't waste it by letting things slip in that are not in line with God's heart for you both. Don't allow anything or anyone to dictate what your marriage should be like except for God or trusted, God-following, encouraging friends and advice-givers. You are choosing whom to invite into your spiritual privacy and the bond that has been built between you and your spouse. Through discernment, be very particular about where the raindrops of encouragement that you need come from. Be careful with what you choose to fill up the empty spaces of your life. Explore the possibilities of investing in your dream of a great marriage by hiring a life coach or a Christian counselor so you can be a spouse who is emotionally whole and ready to keep building a successful marriage.

As your marriage grows and, together, you face the different issues of life, commit to putting your trust in God's direction: He'll make a pathway. Don't consider walking on this path alone —you are inextricably connected to your spouse, locked into God's love through your promises to each other. Never think you can be un-tangled from this oneness. Can you separate the waves from the sand? Can you part a river from its bed? Never. The two will always go together. Think about your marriage in the same way.

You have come together to create a new reality on God's foundation, and His vision for your future to- together. He provides you with ideas and the possibility of what can take place, but it can only happen if your mind is set on being with your spouse forever. Believe that it is possible. Keep up the roadblocks to anything trying to cause havoc in your marriage. See your marriage in the way that God created it to be—forever.

Building up your relationship is an opportunity gifted to you by your Father. Spend time understanding what has been placed upon you. When you go about building up your relationship, God will provide all the support you need, but you must keep your mindset of God being able to do anything, even when it seems impossible. When you do this, you'll conduct yourself God's way. You'll have the right kind of attitude to attract the right kind of change agent. You'll also have the right confidence to face any challenge. Just like a fish lives in water, dwell and live in your marriage. Be patient in constructing your house according to the plans that have been laid before you. These blueprints are not just something that showed up out of the blue. They have been created by the Master Designer, and He knows what is required to raise a house that cannot be destroyed.

Every house is built by someone, but the builder of all things is God. Now Moses was faithful in [the administration of] all God's house, [but only] as a ministering servant, [his ministry serving] as a testimony of the things which were to be spoken afterward [the revelation to come in Christ]; but Christ is faithful as a Son over His [Father's] house. And we are His house if we hold fast our confidence and sense of triumph in our hope [in Christ].

— – HEBREWS 3:4–6 (AMP)

You possess the ability to do anything if it is done through a heart that is patient. Like Moses, put in the work as a ministering servant. Seek understanding about the mission, and be an active participant. Anything that is worth having is worth putting in the work to have it. Go the extra mile to remain connected. Get motivated about your marriage, be a reflection of God's goodness, and be consistent in your willingness to transition to the next, better phase of your relationship. Even dripping water will eventually create an impression in the rock below it. Be consistent. The transformation of your marriage does not take place the first time you invest in it; it happens over time—sometimes a very long time—but only if you are consistent. Align yourself with the things that will help your marriage grow and with nothing that won't.

The more you believe in your marriage, the deeper you will cement yourself in your relationship. Plant your roots deep by the rivers of life and find nourishment and balance. The deeper the roots go, the taller the tree grows, the more branches are produced, the more fruit appears. Commit yourself to becoming a fruit-producing machine. The more good fruit you sow, the more good fruit you will grow. Push your roots deep into the peace and understanding of God, and have an open and gentle heart. Construct it correctly in the truth and design of its Creator. Receive His wisdom, and build a protective shield around your relationship so that no storm will be able to tear it down.

SPEAK LIFE OVER YOUR MARRIAGE

A marriage is a spiritual thing with a divine connection to the one who created it. With your marriage built on God's holy Word, you can use your authority to speak His promises into existence. He is the author of life, and when you speak good things over your marriage, you speak life into it.

There are twenty-four hours in a day, seven days a week, and fifty-two weeks in a year, and in every minute of those days, weeks, and years, you have the opportunity to speak life. Listen to God's words of life, and let them motivate you to do your best. Talk with your Heavenly Father, and express your thoughts about the direction of your marriage. When you're with others, your words pertaining to your marriage should be positive. Even if your spouse is not present, be the light and build up your marital immune system—the readiness to fight off any incoming infection and the health to build your marriage. It is vital that you do not make light of the power of your words or even of your thoughts. Out of the heart, the mouth speaks. Check your heart. Focus on what God sees. Learn how to place a guard over your mouth. Every day, you can avoid saying anything negative about something that impacts your life and only choose to say what's positive, thus preserving your marriage.

It is not a coincidence that God gave you two ears and one mouth. When you spend more time listening than talking, you can listen to your thoughts and filter them before they come out of your mouth. Ask the Father where each negative thought originates from so you can apply His truth to it. This will build your relationship with God and mature you. As you keep training yourself up, you will find yourself choosing words carefully instead of letting everything out. Your speech about your holy union should contain much wisdom, and the life in your words will help stabilize your relationship. Marriages can be destroyed by negative words. I have never heard of anyone's marriage falling apart if they were consistent in speaking life into their relationship. When you speak about your marriage, communicate as if God the Father is present and listening in. Never sink to the side of lies and darkness with your words.

> Do not give the devil an opportunity [to lead you into sin by holding a grudge, or nurturing anger, or harboring resentment, or cultivating bitterness]. ... Do not let unwholesome [foul, profane, worthless, vulgar] words ever come out of your mouth, but only such speech as is good for building up others, according to the need and the occasion, so that it will be a blessing to those who hear [you speak].
>
> — – EPHESIANS 4:27, 29 (AMP)

It has been proven that what other people say about your marriage is not the same thing that God says. People who are on the outside looking in are going to have their thoughts and opinions pertaining to what your marriage should look like. They will communicate what they do and do not agree with when it comes to being a godly spouse, but the basis of their points of view can often come from what has taken place in their lives. My recommendation is that you do what my grandmother told me years ago: eat the meat and spit out the bones.

Chew and meditate on the things you find beneficial and discard the rest because it's contrary to what you believe. Guard your position in your marriage when talking to others. Don't conform to what they believe is true unless it's lined up with the Word. Conform together to what the Word of God speaks about your relationship.

Remember, unity is a strength. When there is teamwork and collaboration, wonderful things can be achieved.

Dream big, and chase after the dream. Expect the best for your marriage. When you said your marriage vows, you made a declaration of purpose. You said you were committed to making your dream a reality. You will face some tough times in your marriage, but it is through weathering those tough times that you develop the most. Anything worth having is worth working through together. Declare over yourself that you have a canopy of protection that's designed to protect your relationship. Declare that your marriage has value. Speak your vision over your marriage. Vision works with spiritual intellect, and your spoken words will influence you to manage your relationship with God's way.

Destructive people can be used by the devil to speak death over your marriage just because they are jealous that they can't have a marriage as good as yours. Their negative words can damage your connection with your spouse, but you have the authority to speak life against the darkness. God's words are so much more powerful, and when you keep these in your mind and speak only His words of hope and life, your marriage is protected from the destructive plans of the world.

You authorize with your words the way your marriage goes. When you speak words of life over your mar- riage, it makes your spouse feel like they have value in the relationship and like they still matter; they are then willing to fight for your marriage with you to see God's purposes fulfilled. Never take the time that you have with your spouse for granted. Every night before bed, look into your spouse's eyes and tell them you will always be on the same sheet of music. By doing this, you are reminding the enemy that you are not going to allow him to separate what God has brought together. You are joined together. You will spend your life together. Your destiny is to live in agreement with heaven that your marriage will always be full of His light and His life.

When it comes to talking with your spouse, obedience is better than any sacrifice that could be presented. "Do you think all God wants are sacrifices—empty rituals just for show? He wants you to listen to him! Plain listening is the thing, not staging a lavish religious production" (1 Samuel 15:22 MSG). When God says, "[Speak] only what is helpful for building others up according to their needs, that it may benefit those who listen" (Ephesians 4:29), do it. When He says, "Be quick to listen, slow to speak and slow to become angry" (James 1:19), do it. When he says, "Gracious words are a honeycomb, sweet to the soul and healing to the bones" (Proverbs 16:24), speak graciously.

Your communication should sound as if it is connected to death. It has the purpose of building and breathing life in a dry place. It is like water from your heavenly Father soaking into the dry places. "The Spirit gives life; the flesh counts for nothing. The words I have spoken to you—they are full of the Spirit and life" (John 6:63). The only way your marriage is going to reach its maximum potential is if you allow the Master to direct your relationship and your words and actions in the relationship. Allow positive words to come out of your mouth for the purpose of reinforcing the things that will help your marriage grow.

PRAY OVER YOUR MARRIAGE

We are all a spirit, soul, and body connected to God's spirit at all times. When God makes us one with our spouse, our spirits are joined as well. We are connected to each other at all times. We can feel the presence of our spouse inside. This connection protects and guides us, because when we pray, we are praying with our spirit as if we were talking with God as both of us, not just ourselves.

You are both one with God, reaching for your destiny in Him together. When you pray, the time you spend has extraordinary value. You are praying for an ever-in-creasing oneness with your spouse in God. As Jesus prayed, "I [pray] for [all] those who [will ever] believe and trust in Me through their message, that they all may be one; just as You, Father, are in Me and I in You, that they also may be one in Us" (John 17:20–21 AMP).

When you consistently pray for your marriage, every request has value. Do not be afraid to release your requests out loud so they can reach their destination.

When you do this, you seal the warranty that protects your relationship—the warranty connected to God's promises and His will for your marriage on the day you made your agreement before Him.

Working together as one, your spirit plays a key role in building your relationship. As you pray together in agreement, the force field you create protects you from the forces of evil. "Whatever you bind on earth will be bound in heaven, and whatever you loose on earth will be loosed in heaven. Again, truly I tell you that if two of you agree on earth about anything they ask for, it will be done for them by my Father in heaven" (Matthew 18:18–19). In the place of agreement, everything lines up for you to be successful together. This does not mean that you will not face some adversity. It just means that whatever you face, you possess the capacity to be able to overtake it. Know that the hand of God is upon your marriage and He has a vested interest in it being successful, which is why you have so much power and authority at your disposal when you pray.

Receive Jesus as the head of your relationship. Receive the spirit of God as a gift to communicate with your heavenly Father. The Holy Spirit will open your heart to His desires for your life. Jesus and God the Father are intertwined in oneness, which causes us to believe that it is possible to be intertwined with our spouse and committed to each other. In this place of safety, we are not afraid of making ourselves vulnerable, and we must be a place of safety when our spouse is putting down their guard and allowing us to see their areas of weakness. When they trust us like this, we must be mature enough to handle the pressure that comes with seeing their areas of concern. We must do our part in putting up a shield in prayer that protects them from the fiery darts of destruction.

Always ask God what's required of you. Keep absorbing Scriptures and wise information that can build your relationship. "The word of God is living and active and full of power [making it operative, energizing, and effective]" (Hebrews 4:12 AMP). His Word can mature you and help you grow in character. It provides you with a picture of how to look at the heart of your marriage instead of the tangible things. It helps you develop a gentle spirit, making you more confident and faith-filled. Wield your sword of the Word. "Take the ... sword of the Spirit, which is the word of God" (Ephesians 6:17). You possess the ability to place adversarial things under your feet. Never quit praying over your marriage!

> Working together with Him, we strongly urge you not to receive God's grace in vain [by turning away from sound doctrine and His merciful kindness]. ...
>
> We commend ourselves in every way as servants of God: in great endurance, in sufferings, in hardships, in distresses, ... in sleepless nights, ... in purity and sincerity, in knowledge and spiritual insight, in patience, in kindness, in the Holy Spirit, in genuine love, in [speaking] the word of truth, in the power of God; by the weapons of righteousness for the right hand [like holding the sword to attack] and for the left [like holding the shield to defend], amid glory and dishonor.
>
> — – 2 CORINTHIANS 6:1, 4–8 (AMP)

PROTECT YOUR MARRIAGE

We should train our spirit to be prepared for the fighting and defensive actions we must often take in prayer for our marriage.

> Discipline yourself for the purpose of godliness [keeping yourself spiritually fit]. For physical training is of some value, but godliness (spiritual training) is of value in everything and in every way, since it holds promise for the present life and for the life to come.
>
> — – 1 TIMOTHY 4:7–8 (AMP)

When I say "fight," I never mean fight your spouse! Marriage is about oneness, not two opponents in a boxing ring. If you're fighting with your spouse, don't go against God this way. Don't go back to seeing and doing things the way the world would. "You were following the ways of this world [influenced by this present age], in accordance with the prince of the power of the air (Satan), the spirit who is now at work in the disobedient [the unbelieving, who fight against the purposes of God]" (Ephesians 2:2 AMP). And don't try to control each other. "[Things to Avoid:] What leads to [the un- ending] quarrels and conflicts among you? Do they not come from your [hedonistic] desires that wage war in your [bodily] members [fighting for control over you]?" (James 4:1 AMP). Only people who are immature in their thinking fight against someone who has been anointed and appointed to fight alongside them.

Fight for oneness, for teamwork, for togetherness. This is how you deal with problems in your marriage. Your spouse is in your marriage to be in your corner as you fight in the ring called life, encouraging you to keep going and guiding you as you engage in the fight. Do the same for your spouse. The true enemy, the father of lies, fights against you both. He is set on destroying your marriage and your life, and he will try to make you pull away from the person who has your best interests at heart. Don't let him win! "Jesus said to them, 'Any kingdom that is divided against itself is being laid waste; and no city or house divided against itself will [continue to] stand'" (Matthew 12:25 AMP).

The enemy also wants to separate you from the relationship that you have with God. Train yourself up and learn how to fight by becoming a true disciple of Jesus:

- Memorize the Word and let its life flow through you.
- Always listen and obey God.
- Reject any words or thoughts that don't align with the Word of God.
- "Be unceasing and persistent in prayer" (1 Thessalonians 5:17 AMP).
- "In every situation [no matter what the circumstances], be thankful and continually give thanks to God" (v. 18 AMP).
- "[Let] the God of peace Himself sanctify you through and through [that is, separate you from profane and vulgar things, make you pure and whole

and undamaged—consecrated to Him—set apart for His purpose]" (v. 23 AMP).

Your marriage is valuable. Prove it by putting in the work to make it better. Every good thing is built one step at a time, and you can learn so much when it comes to fighting the enemy. Your relationship is covered under God's spiritual umbrella when you live life His way. You'll learn that the enemy never comes up with any new ways of fighting. Invest in getting to know his strategies. Understand that it's his goal to separate you from your spouse. He's the opponent, not your loved one. Recognize his attacks together and, side by side, fight him back.

The spirit of God fills you and pulls you deeper into love. The more time you spend with God, the more you will radiate His energy, and the more you will love your spouse. Your strategy is to let the goodness and kindness of God overflow in your marriage. Ask Him to assist you in working on the areas that need to be improved. The spirit of God is a perfect gift that will reflect His greatness in your marriage and in everything you do.

Let God always have the first and last word. Make Him the authority that supersedes your relationship. See things His way. Choose His way. React His way. There is nothing like being in a relationship where you both have godly behavior and only desire to be a blessing. "Love [that unselfishly seeks the best for others] builds up and encourages others to grow [in wisdom]" (1 Corinthians 8:1 AMP).

You are both the gatekeepers of your marriage. You only grant access to the things of God, gifts that establish a healthy link between you both—like words of encouragement. Remember that words are weighty. For example, I have communicated with people who spent time in jail, who said that if someone had been available to encourage them and provide guidance, then maybe that would have helped prevent them from going down the wrong path.

[For my hope is] that their hearts may be encouraged as they are knit together in [unselfish] love, so that they may have all the riches that come from the full assurance of understanding [the joy of sal- vation], resulting in a true [and more intimate] knowledge of the mystery of God, that is, Christ.

— – COLOSSIANS 2:2 (AMP)

A consistent voice of encouragement is like the con- sistent consumption of water. "Encourage and comfort one another and build up one another, just as you are doing" (1 Thessalonians 5:11 AMP).

Always do everything God's way, no matter what your opin-ions are or how different you are from your spouse. Learn how to appreciate the things you have each brought to the relationship and use them to follow God's instructions as a team. "The Lord will guide you always; he will satisfy your needs in a sun-scorched land and will strengthen your frame. You will be like a well watered garden, like a spring whose waters never fail" (Isaiah 58:11). When we do things His way, it will work out in our favor because we give Him the control. We will bear His fruit. Your marriage has been created to be a producer of things that will be beneficial to the world, including your wisdom on marriage learned in the trenches. This means that on a consistent basis, you should be doing things to help your marriage develop so God's light can shine through it.

"Jesus declared, 'I am the bread of life. Whoever comes to me will never go hungry, and whoever believes in me will never be thirsty'" (John 6:35). Through your relationship with Him, He will make it possible to fulfill your desires and satisfy any urges only inside your marriage. Your marriage is enough. Your main sexual desire should only ever be to have a more intimate relationship with your spouse. Without Jesus, this is impossible. You'd be like the zombie from the TV show *The Walking Dead*. A marriage that's in the will of God is satisfying if you are persistent about having a great marriage. Take your desires and place them in the correct place—in the presence of your heavenly Father—and know that He will ensure that your desires for your marriage will come to pass.

Some Christians seem to have more peace and spiritual authority than others, and this is because they are more obedient to God's ways. When He speaks, they jump. You might be able to live life like a fast car, but if you don't obey the speed limit, God can pull you over.

Deal with disruptions in your marriage the same way—if anything tries to get past your rules of peace and agreement, you have the authority to "pull it over" and take it off the road.

Getting your marriage in alignment brings about peace and protection for your relationship.

God wants your relationship to stay peaceful and not become disruptive. What force or power is causing this? What's making it grow? To get it to stop, you must remove its power. Agree together to dwell in peace. Use your authority to say no to your anger and negativity. Speak words of peace and encouragement. Conflict is connected to the enemy, and his objective is for you to dwell in a miserable marriage. Settle in your mind and in your heart that you are going to connect to peace, and in the end, you'll win. Take back what the enemy has stolen from you. Kill his hope of trying to derail you and destroy any access he has to you. You'll only be able to do this through God's power, might, and strength He has given to your marriage.

Trust and believe that you can change a situation together. Rejoice in advance for your victory. Fight for the opportunity to take possession of peace. Know that you are blessed because you are called to be a peacemaker in your relationship. The Holy Spirit will give you positive ideas to help build your relationship and keep you away from hopelessness. The peace you experience will have you feeling as if everything in your life is a blessing.

Conflict and confusion cannot dwell in the presence of the Father's holiness, so the more your marriage is a reflection of Him and is connected to Him, the less confusion can dwell in it. Spend time with the God of peace. Build your faith in His presence.

At some point in your marriage, you will find that you have become someone who empowers peace—the result of years of faith in God's promises and trusting that He gives you the best tools to grow your marriage with. You'll know what you have influence over and use it, thus becoming one who creates a sense of harmony in your marriage.

INVEST IN YOUR MARRIAGE

God wants your marriage to be as fruitful as possible. Seek out an understanding on how to build your marriage in an effective way. Ask Him how to invest in your marriage.

You got married for life. Just like some stocks take a long time to give a return, your effort in investing in your marriage in not in vain. You'll eventually see your return. Fill your heart and mind with His Word, and build on it every day with God. Never doubt what He gives you. Let His Word push you to be great. Just like a stockbroker, watch your investments. Keep what works, and offload what doesn't. Learn from Him. As you do this regularly, you will find your marriage becoming easier to manage and operating at full capacity.

The efforts that you put forth in your marriage are not in vain. "Let us throw off everything that hinders and the sin that so easily entangles. And let us run with perseverance the race marked out for us" (Hebrews 12:1). Our life in Christ can be like an ongoing college class. We listen, study to show ourselves approved, and take regular tests. Be a student of life who is out to receive the best grade possible. Some tests will be difficult, but God says, "My grace is sufficient for you, for my power is made perfect in weakness" (2 Corinthians 12:9).

Remain focused, and do not get distracted by the people who

don't follow Christ. Your grade comes from your heavenly instructor. He has put together a lesson plan and provided you with the material for a specific purpose. It is up to you to do your part in investing the time to study it all. Take what has been given and apply it to your marriage. Pay attention in class, complete all your assignments, do your homework, and prepare yourself for the test that's coming. You'll be graded on your efforts.

Do your part. As you learn and carry out what you learn, you build your confidence. You walk by the faith that you have in your relationship. You start to feel ready for anything. And you are. As Paul said, "I eagerly expect and hope that I will in no way be ashamed, but will have sufficient courage so that now as always Christ will be exalted in my body, whether by life or by death" (Philippians 1:20).

CHAPTER 8

Don't Quit!

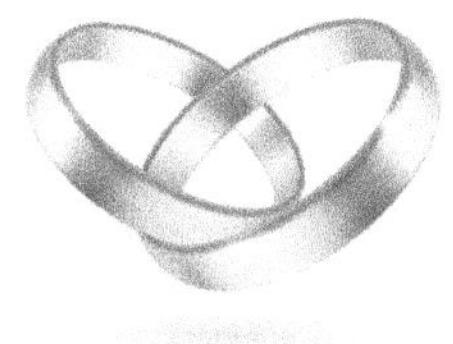

At the proper time, we will reap a harvest if we do not give up.
– Galatians 6:9

QUIT, verb transitive

1. To have done with; to cease from; to stop; hence, to
   depart from; to leave; to forsake; ...

Quitimplies a going without intention of return, a final and absolute abandonment.

– Webster's Dictionary 1913[1]

The park is one of the best places to go to obtain peace of mind, especially early in the morning. You can relax and enjoy the scenery of God's creation. No one is demanding you to do something. You don't have to be ready for anything. You are in a place of peace. Maybe right now, your marriage demands your attention or your effort, but with God, a time will come when you can relax and enjoy simply being in it. You can have peace within your marriage. It can be healthy. It can be what you say it will be. It all depends on what you are willing to invest in it.

REJOICE IN YOUR MARRIAGE

Rejoicing in your marriage, no matter what it looks like today, guards against the hopelessness that can make it fail. A wall of joy cannot be penetrated. The enemy looks to the left and to the right to find a soft spot through which he can enter and cause decay, but joy keeps us settled in peace and strength. "Rejoice in the Lord! It is no trouble for me to write the same things to you again, and it is a safeguard for you" (Philippians 3:1). Having a heart that consistently rejoices in what has been given allows us to see things as God does. We then focus our attention on what will come to pass in faith rather than on current circumstances. Do you believe you have been equipped with the appropriate tools to take you to the place where you believe you belong? You have, but you must make the right choices to get there.

Taking responsibility for every choice you make shows that you are preparing for great things. So many gifts have been stored up for you, and one of the biggest, most powerful gifts is joy. Believe it. Speak it. Be excited about what is about to take place in your marriage. It won't start tomorrow because it starts the moment you believe it is possible; then, God takes your possibility and turns it into reality. We must give Him an inkling of hope, a mustard seed of faith, to work with and develop. Hope helps you to keep going and makes space for the building and expansion of your marriage. Have hope for your marriage to excel and prosper. Stop engaging in your marriage as if you are a victim, and start operating in it, knowing that you have the upper hand against hopelessness.

> Consider it pure joy, my brothers and sisters, whenever you face trials of many kinds because you know that the testing of your faith produces perseverance. Let perseverance finish its work so that you may be mature and complete, not lacking any- thing. If any of you lacks wisdom, you should ask God, who gives generously to all without finding fault, and it will be given to you. But when you ask, you must believe and not doubt because the one who doubts is like a wave of the sea, blown and tossed by the wind.
>
> — – JAMES 1:2–6, EMPHASIS MINE

CREATE A JOY-FILLED MARRIAGE

Make it your mission to create an atmosphere in your marriage that you love dwelling in—one of joy. I'm not talking about happiness. Joy is different. Happiness is more about feelings of contentment when good things happen to you, whereas joy is about making good things happen. It's about choosingto rejoice, to delight in, to be glad.

One of your assignments is to find joy in your marriage. Having the joy of the Lord has nothing to do with you being happy, because it doesn't rely on favorable circumstances. It is based on a godly choice and not a worldly emotion. Having joy in your marriage is about finding satisfaction in something that was created to be a blessing.

Finding joy in a marriage is very powerful, and it can dominate your thoughts in the best way possible. Open your heart and mind to living this way. Dominate the atmosphere, not the person created to be your blessing. Let God pull your thoughts toward available opportunities for joy. These areas are waiting for you to show up with your spiritual equipment, ready to expand and grow in them, ready to put forth maximum effort into growing good fruit. You have the authority and dominion to choose joy every time. You have been given the jurisdiction to choose the life you desire to have, and joy is what can power it. "Therefore my heart is glad and my glory [my innermost self] rejoices; my body too will dwell [confidently] in safety" (Acts 2:26 AMP).

Give your marriage your undivided attention. Learn as much as you can about God's view of marriage. Find the heartbeat of your marriage, and let the Holy Spirit keep pushing you and motivating you to desiring more. God has so much more ready and waiting, and it will bring more fulfillment and satisfaction than you thought possible. Learn how to get excited about what God the Father has given you, and ask Him for a plan that will allow you to take possession of the blessings awaiting you both.

KEEP ON GIVING

Be receptive to the direction of the Holy Spirit. He will guide you in how to conduct yourself to please your spouse. Focus on being willing to learn instead of the outcome of your efforts, because you won't get it right every time, and your spouse will pick up on your actions being more about your expectations than about loving the way Christ does. Having the right heart motive affects how a person receives your gift.

The effort you put into giving and serving demonstrates your desire to give with no expectations. Your spouse will recognize how much time and thought you invest in putting each gift together, whether it's a movie night, an electronic item, a piece of jewelry, or a weekend away without the kids. If you present a gift to your spouse and you are off in meeting their expectations, work on understanding your spouse better so you can get it right next time. Have an honest, peaceful discussion about the gift, and don't let yourself get- fended. Gift-giving is never about you and always about the receiver, so it's simply about learning what would make your spouse feel most loved. You might make the mistake of giving what you would enjoy the most. You can't get offended about getting it wrong. Stay humble and keep learning and trying. Your time is valuable, and you want to ensure that your efforts are not in vain. As you build upon this, you will find yourself becoming consistent at striking the mark and investing wisely in your marriage.

Pay close attention to the transition of the relationship to make the appropriate adjustments in your giving. Your spouse's desires and needs will change, and the thing that at one time was important to them no longer holds the value it once held. If you are not paying attention to the transition, you will find yourself investing in something your spouse doesn't want or need anymore, and your gift won't be received with the same enthusiasm.

When it comes to giving gifts, shift your focus from your spouse's reaction to loving like Jesus. His only concern is how the Father will react. Will He be pleased with your efforts and the heart behind your giving, or are you only giving so you can get something out of it? Will the Father say He is well pleased with the attitude of your heart (Matthew 3:17)? Look forward to giving, using it as a way to create change, and help fill an empty spot in your spouse's life. When you are focused on improving your spouse's life with your gifts, it removes all selfishness and desire to control with your giving. It is like investing in the stock market. What authority do you have in controlling how the stock market operates? You do your homework and invest in the stocks you believe will give you the best return on your investment, but you can't control how they will do. For the best return, keep investing in your marriage according to what the Holy Spirit says. Trust Him. The return that you can receive will exceed your expectations. You'll have a heart that's fulfilled, and you'll be fired up about your marriage.

Focus on being a blessing. Do not concern yourself with what you are going to receive. Place your trust in God, knowing that He will deal with the heart of your marriage. Respect His process, knowing that Jesus is interceding for your relationship. "Christ

Jesus who died—more than that, who was raised to life—is at the right hand of God and is also interceding for us. Who shall separate us from the love of Christ?" (Romans 8:34–35). Humble yourself about the things that you believe you deserve, and be more excited about the opportunity to invest in your marriage. The God you serve is not like man. He understands what it is going to take to get the required results. Listen to Him and follow His advice.

Allow God to show you how much you can enjoy your marriage. Do not allow anyone to tell you that you can- not enjoy your life with your spouse. There is so much strength in knowing that the spirit of God is present among and in you both. He is working on your hearts and on your behalf as your teammate, doing His part so you can keep running the race with your eyes fixed on Him instead of trying to look good.

PATIENCE

Waiting on God is like waiting for an oven to preheat. As your relationship goes through the process of preheating, everything within comes together and works together for the purpose of producing something amaz- ing. Learn to preheat your relation- ship by doing what- ever God says. Believe that your actions will generate a reward based on your efforts. Nothing does the heart more good than to look at your spouse's face and see love there because you believed in God's promises for your marriage and kept going.

You have to believe that your marriage will last until "death do you part." You have to know that you can en- joy your spouse and the life that has been given to you.

Remaining patient will cause you to lock in on what has been spoken and trust it will develop and produce over time. Your productivity in your marriage is connected to the foresight you have for your relationship. Keep sending your roots deeper into God. He is the key to remaining calm and not allowing things to become a distraction from what He sees. Never believe that what you have started does not have the capacity to make it.

Build up enough courage to take an honest evaluation of your relationship because you contain the power and authority to speak change into it. Never doubt that what's in your heart has the potential to come to pass.

Identify the issues within it, and get to work. Approach it all with joy, knowing God's got you. "'Have faith in God,' Jesus answered. 'Truly I tell you, if anyone says to this mountain, "Go, throw yourself into the sea," and does not doubt in their heart but believes that what they say will happen, it will be done for them'" (Mark 11:22– 23). When you trust how big God is, you'll be willing to put all your effort into your marriage. Push past the idea that you can't make your marriage work. Don't let your doubts talk you out of having a great marriage. Believe that all things are possible, and be patient enough to wait for it to come to pass.

Have confidence in who you are and who is in you, and this will give you peace in your relationship. When you're resting in Him, you can communicate with your spouse from a place of peace. You are able to think through a process and evaluate all aspects of a situation without feeling like you have to rush to an answer. You owe it to yourself to take your time to ensure that you get it right. You have the capacity to have better intentions and make better choices. Being calm helps you appreciate and enjoy each moment. The Father is not slow in giving you what your relationship needs—He's already given it all, and now it's up to you to receive it and activate it so it can be all that it can be.

Everything that happens in your marriage is an opportunity. Will you change or quit? Change the way you think. Waste nothing; use every opportunity to engage, be present, and do better. Your marriage is not a wishing well where you disconnect yourself from your ability to do something and say that now that you're married, things just happen, and you're powerless to stop them.

Marriage is a three-stranded cord that only works when you are all on the same team—both of you with God and with each other. Be encouraged. Continue to believe that things are coming together—you'll understand your spouse better, and you'll stay committed to your vows.

The more you obtain understanding about what you have, the more God will build your knowledge and trust in His actions. Be patient in waiting for what has been promised. Follow His standard, and work on your areas of imperfection one step at a time. As you do this, you'll build your confidence in what you can achieve.

Stressing over things that have no impact leads to bitterness on both sides. It stops you from wanting to nurture and protect each other and puts you on opposing sides. Timely detection of any type of bitterness is vital to the survival of your marriage.

Watch your spouse carefully for any signs of unhappiness and address it. Do not just address the big stuff. I recommend that you talk about anything upsetting during a time of peace to ensure that it does not develop into something later that ends up getting out of control. Make it your personal business to address the areas in your life that need your attention. It is okay to be on top of speaking life into your marriage and making sure you are both on the same page.

LONG SUFFERING

Understand your times of long-suffering in your marriage—"bearing injuries or provocation for a long time; patient; not easily provoked" (Webster's 1913). Long-suffering is like what you do when you have an injury. The first thing you do is observe the severity of the injury and determine how you are going to take care of it. Once the appropriate diagnosis has taken place, you mentally prepare yourself to go through the time period the doctor has given you for getting better. Looking ahead, you prepare yourself for long-suffering—you see yourself dealing with pain and inconvenience as it comes. If you are not able to find a quick healing, you become frustrated and annoyed. You feel like you are trapped, but you know that the injury will eventually heal. You are patient in waiting for things to turn around in your favor. You know frustration, self-pity, and anger won't help you heal any faster, and they could even delay your healing.

Yes, you will have painful moments. No, you are not willing to remain under the umbrella of pain. You are patient, shining light on what's important to you by following the doctor's instructions to the letter and trusting in the outcome. This is the way of effectively building on what's important. Suffering in your marriage hurts, but keep following God's ways of handling it instead of checking out. When you check out, you seem lazy or disinterested, as if your marriage is not all that important to you. If you see value in it, you will put forth the effort and time to ensure that it is successful, no matter how much pain you are in. You are willing to do what's required. So the question you should ask yourself is how valuable your marriage is to you. Learn to run from the things destroying your marriage and to the one who will build it.

God has already prepared every blessing for your marriage, and you will receive it all in due time and in due season. This is confirmation that your season is appointed to come to pass. Deal with each pressure together. Resist the efforts of the enemy to tear you apart.

Build your marriage to be an example to others. Couples are looking for good role models who can advise them on their own marital struggles and how to not give up. You can be there for them.

Anything that's worth having is worth going into combat for. You are equipped for battle. This battle is not going to be short; it might last for an extended period of time—but God has given you sustainable grace to endure the battle.

> I ... beseech you to walk worthy of the calling with which
> you were called, with all lowliness and gentleness, with

longsuffering, bearing with one another in love, endeavoring to keep the unity of the Spirit in the bond of peace. There is … one God and Father of all, who is above all, and through all, and in you all.

— – EPHESIANS 4: 1–4, 6 (NKJV)

Prepare for long-suffering, but also prepare for battle. Fight for peace and a unified approach to life. Stay as one through any disagreement. Appreciate the pro- cess and what you are both learning through it. Keep your marriage in high regard. You have a treasured relationship that will produce a harvest when you stick with it for the long haul. God has the patience to see your marriage become fruitful. Ask Him to fill you with His patience: "The Lord God, merciful and gracious, long-suffering and abundant in goodness" (Exodus 34:6 NKJV). Don't be unaware or ignorant of His own long-suffering with you: "Do you despise the riches of His goodness, forbearance, and longsuffering, not knowing that the goodness of God leads you to repentance?" (Ro- mans 2:4 NKJV).

The Father knows what marriage can and cannot accomplish. He only requires that we trust the process of being patient and long-suffering and waiting on His instruction. Do not pass up the opportunity to have a great marriage. Listen and obey, and He will teach you how to build an indestructible marriage grounded on the Word of God.

Long-suffering keeps you excited about what is going to come and content about what is taking place at the present moment. It means you can soon be connected in a deeper way to your spouse. Keep being a person of peace, and your marriage will become one of peace as well. It is not about what you suffer through that makes things better. It's not about your past experiences. It's about having the right kind of attitude about your relationship when you are suffering. Maturity is knowing that everything is going to work out in God's favor, be- cause all things exist based on who God is, and everything He does works out.

> He who searches the hearts knows what the mind of the Spirit is because the Spirit intercedes [before God] on behalf of God's people in accordance with God's will. And we know [with great confidence] that God [who is deeply concerned about us] causes all things to work together [as a plan] for good for those who love God, to those who are called according to His plan and purpose.
>
> — – ROMANS 8:27–28 (AMP)

God did not tell us to be patient so we'd suffer. He knows better times are ahead. We can learn how to trust the inner man and reject inappropriate emotional decisions, and once we're in sync with God's way of doing things, we obtain access to the things we're waiting on. We get to see what the eyes cannot naturally see, hear what our ears cannot naturally hear, and think thoughts uncorrupted by an unguarded heart. We get to be on guard and examine everything that tries to enter in. We have no better armor than to be clothed in Christ.

Long-suffering can be freeing because we learn how to live unoffended. We learn how to live in a place of rest no matter what is going on around us. We trust our Maker. We become free to be who we were created to be. Our weak areas are strengthened. Our expectations are turned into hopes. We serve out of a heart of love instead of our neediness. We take off the mask and become honest and vulnerable. We allow truth to be in control, smoothing out the areas of imperfection. For all this to happen, we must be long-suffering and patient.

HOPE

You must have hope. You must believe that your marriage was created to be great. Settle in your heart that your marriage is covered by God. "Faith is the substance of thing hoped for, the evidence of things not seen" (- Hebrews 11:1). Your marriage and how you face turbulent times are a reflection of your faith. You are both connected to the substance of your faith, and He is the great stabilizer, strong enough to hold up the marriage. Identify who and what you believe in. Your marriage will be all it can be because He is its foundation, its builder, and its center of hope.

We place our faith in Jesus and our trust in the truth and power of the Word. His promises are the target we can shoot toward. Faith is that force field that protects your marriage from things that come against you. Faith is that Jiminy Cricket is on your shoulder to remind you to make the right choices. Your faith gives you the courage to keep going when you face obstacles that seem impossible. "Without faith, it is impossible to [walk with

God and] please Him, for whoever comes [near] to God must [necessarily] believe that God exists and that He rewards those who [earnestly and diligently] seek Him" (He- brews 11:6 AMP). If you do not believe that His Word is true, you believe that He can't deal with your situation. Your faith in the Word of God communicates to the Father that you have a vision for your marriage. Your hope is alive, and you trust Him to light the way. You also trust Him to expose things that can bring harm to your marriage. The faith God gives is indestructible and undefeatable. Walk in it. Hold it close, and you cannot and will not lose to the adversary, who is out to destroy your relationship.

You are going to need faith in your marriage to be able to get over the hump. "Faith comes from hearing [what is told], and what is heard comes by the [preach- ing of the] message concerning Christ" (Romans 10:17 AMP). Stay in the Word, and your faith will not waver. Faith never stops moving in your marriage, working at all times for it to be impactful. Faith gives you the energy to be consistent, to keep going through each situa-tion until you get it right. Faith is both an offensive and defensive machine that's prepared to go the distance, and you have access to it all. The spoken Word of God builds your relationship and your mindset of what is available to you. If you are able to visualize everything good in your mind, you have the power to cause it to come to pass in your marriage. Your strength is tied to your faith that God is bigger than any problem you face.

You are now part of God's family of God the Father, Son, and Holy Spirit. You are one with your spouse and one with Him. A healthy marriage is fully possible in Him as long as you do not believe something else over that original confession. Your faith keeps you focused and prevents you from straying off the path toward a great marriage.

Build up your mind that you are not going to waver in your faith. Declare that your marriage has no choice but to be successful. I define faith as:

- Forward: The direction you move in
- Action: Things you do
- In: Investments you make
- Trusting: The Word and promises of God
- Him: The resource that fuels the marriage

Faith gives you the confidence to keep moving forward as you place your trust in Him. Always be proac- tive, never reactive. Don't base your actions on what your spouse gives you in return but on what God has put in your heart and on what you vowed at the altar. "Someone may say, 'You [claim to] have faith and I have [good] works; show me your [alleged] faith without the works [if you can], and I will show you my faith by my works [that is, by what I do]'" (James 2:18 AMP). Do what you do based on the Spirit inside you. Follow His blocks of instruction to become successful. When you have your mind-set right, your hope follows. Hope comes from God and not your spouse. You do what He tells you to do, and you can trust the process because God doesn't attach strings to His words—extra weights that weren't authorized to come along for the ride. When you are able to do things from the heart, you can really tap into your inner firm foundation. When you give gifts from a heart that's stable, you look past what your spouse is doing and saying and connect to a Father who is bigger than your issue.

You said vows at the altar, promising to live your life as one with your spouse forever. You promised sacrificial love to the one you love and said you would treat them with love and honor them forever because of their value to you. That value has not changed, and if it feels like it has, you need to let God transform your heart. Jesus gave His life so you could be one with the Father. His sacrificial love for you is priceless and leaves an everlasting imprint on your heart. You have the same opportunity for sacrificial love with your spouse. When you treat your spouse as a valuable and priceless person, you get access to your spouse's heart.

Your marriage was created to be incorruptible and inexhaustible, like the Energizer bunny that's designed to keep going and never run out of energy. The only way this is possible is if you stay plugged into the source that sustains your relationship. Never believe that within a certain time period, you are going to experience something that will cause your marriage to fall apart. When your marriage is built upon the rock, it will hold you up through everything.

Craft your mind around the idea that there is nothing that you cannot do as a couple. You were each created differently, and you may each look at a thing in a particular way, but you must always view your marriage through God's eyes, as a blessing and not as a curse. Act like it's a blessing too. Concentrate on always doing the right thing to the best of your ability until it becomes second nature. Become consistent in trusting God to guide you through your marriage. The more you trust Him, the more consistent you will become in speaking life over your marriage.

Stand firm and hold [tightly] to the traditions which you were taught, whether by word of mouthor by letter from us.

Now may our Lord Jesus Christ Himself and God our Father, who has loved us and given us everlasting comfort and encouragement and the good [well-founded] hope [of salvation] by His grace, comfort, encourage, and strengthen your hearts [keeping them steadfast and on course] in every good work and word.

— – 2 THESSALONIANS 2:15–17 (AMP)

It is imperative that you do not lose hope or faith in the words you are confessing. Your faith in His Word will have no choice but to manifest itself, and you will find yourself rejoicing in the Lord when it does. Your words of hope spoken on a consistent basis produce a hope chest or treasure box ready for your next season of marriage. Only you can determine the value of the box based on what you put into it. Speak into it the future reality of what you believe today.

Benefits are attached to your hope and faith. "In Him also we have received an inheritance [a destiny—we were claimed by God as His own], having been predestined (chosen, appointed beforehand) according to the purpose of Him who works everything in agreement with the counsel and design of His will" (Ephesians 1:11 AMP).

An inheritance from God supersedes any reward a person on earth can ever provide. He looks at you as an investment, and He takes pleasure in investing in your life and marriage because you are now His child. He has set you up to inherit (take ownership of, operate in, move forward in victory) blessings for your marriage. God understands what your relationship needs. Become like a little child who comes to his or her parents seeking answers. Your union is a gift from God, and He can clear away any confusion you have about it. He has armed your marriage with all the ammo that's needed to build it beautifully, and you are prepared for battle. Continue to expect that you will come out on the other side with your faculties intact. Stay on guard and ready to take on anything that's out to attack your relationship.

You want to ensure that you are placing the correct items in your treasure chest. Things of no value have no business being there, and if you insist on adding them, your treasure chest will convert to a clutter box—a junk box that makes it difficult to find what you need to help grow your marriage. Your treasure chest is a reminder of everything you appreciate about your connection with your spouse, displaying hope for your union. Dream about things that cause the interest rate to go up in your marriage. Place a ceiling on how much value you give the opinions of others. The priceless things in life originate from a place that's priceless.

Every year money loses its value based on inflation— it doesn't develop or add value over time. But patience and love can and will add value to your marriage. Love's foundational value is connected to its source. Your love is controlled by the Holy Spirit if you focus on Him as your treasure.

> Do not store up for yourselves [material] treasures on earth, where moth and rust destroy, and where thieves break in and steal. But store up for your- selves treasures in heaven, where neither moth nor rust destroys, and where thieves do not break in and steal; for where your treasure is, there your heart [your wishes, your desires; that on which your life centers] will be also.
>
> — – MATTHEW 6:19–21 (AMP)

When unbelievers are confined to the things that they believe are possible, their "treasure" is eaten up by the issues of life that they allow to affect them. Earthly hope will lose its value and eventually become invaluable for your relationship. Find the things that should be stored up in heavenly places, and let your hope dwell there.

Grace to you and peace [inner calm and spiritual well-being] from God our Father and the Lord Jesus Christ.

> Blessed and worthy of praise be the God and Father of our Lord Jesus Christ, who has blessed us with every spir- itual blessing in the heavenly realms in Christ, just as [in His love] He chose us in Christ [actually selected us for Himself as His own] before the foundation of the world.
>
> — – EPHESIANS 1:2–4 (AMP)

This is where your mind should rest. This is where hope can grow and expand freely. This location is protected, and it is surrounded by the right kind of rich soil that causes your relationship to grow, thereby increasing the value of the items in your hope chest or treasure box over time. Each time you go to the treasure box, you can feel joy in seeing the increase in your investment.

It is never about what you can receive from the marriage that blesses you but what you invest in the marriage from a heart that trusts and listens to the Father. Obtaining wisdom is a key component that increases the value of the marriage.

[For my hope is] that their hearts may be encouraged as they are knit together in [unselfish] love, so that they may have all the riches that come from the full assurance of understanding [the joy of sal- vation], resulting in a true [and more intimate] knowledge of the mystery of God, that is, Christ, in whom are hidden all the treasures of wisdom and knowledge [regarding the word and purposes of God].

— COLOSSIANS 2:2–3 (AMP)

Invoke the power of love, and use wisdom in how you function in your marriage. Your marriage should be like a deep cup that's always ready to receive more wisdom. Build your foundation around who He is. Trust Him. Be- lieve in the outcome.

DON'T QUIT!

As a spouse who believes in the institute of the marriage, you desire to dwell in a place that's holy and that will keep you satisfied. Isaiah 58:11 contains revelation knowledge that supports this hope:

> The Lord will continually guide you,
>> And satisfy your soul in scorched and dry places,
>> And give strength to your bones;
>> And you will be like a watered garden,
>> And like a spring of water whose waters do not fail.
>> And your people will rebuild the ancient ruins;
>> You will raise up and restore the age-old foundations
> [of buildings that have been laid waste];
>> You will be called Repairer of the Breach,
>> Restorer of Streets with Dwellings.
>
> — – ISAIAH 58:11–12 (AMP)

Applying this Scripture to your marriage, the Father is saying that as long as you are open to what He is able to do, He will guide you and help you build your relationship. He will satisfy your soul (mind, will, and emotions). Allow the Word of God to be poured over your marriage on a continual basis. The dry areas will come to life based on His power, replenishing the relationship. Build the proper nutrition around your roots. It will give it the strength to live in any type of weather and reach its full potential.

When you look at a young sapling, you can never tell how tall it will grow, but the more you nurture it, the more growth you will see. It's the same with the development of your marriage. If you do not give up on the process over the years, you will see the reward of your persistent, hard work.

YOU CAN DO IT!

Find a way to work together in order to unify in oneness. Keep working together with the goal of staying together. Your marriage is a thought-out plan, and the goal is to be able to grow together and never quit. Invest in staying in the fight and not separating under any condition. Build the marriage on your agreement on this. "When you see it in your mind, you can hold it in your hand" (Steve Harvey). The vision you have for your marriage can become a reality if you come to a permanent place of agreement.

Know that God has your best interests at heart. Get in a place of agreement where God is first, and everything else falls in line after Him. He has said that once you are in agreement with His Word, there isn't anything He will hold back from you:

I joyfully delight in the law of God in my inner self [with my new nature].

— – ROMANS 7:22 (AMP)

[We] have the first fruits of the Spirit [a joyful indication of the blessings to come]. ... For in this hope, we were saved [by faith]. But hope [the object of] which is seen is not hope. For who hopes for what he already sees? But if we hope for what we do not see, we wait eagerly for it with patience and com- posure.

— ROMANS 8:23–25 (AMP)

Get excited! Being in agreement captures the attention of the Father. When you walk in agreement, there isn't a question of if it is going to be done but about being excited that it is already done and in the process of becoming visible.

Praise the Lord! (Hallelujah!)
Blessed [fortunate, prosperous, and favored by God] is the man who fears the Lord [with awe-inspired reverence and worships Him with obedience],
Who delights greatly in His commandments.
His descendants will be mighty on earth;
The generation of the upright will be blessed.
Wealth and riches are in his house,
And his righteousness endures forever.

— – PSALM 112:1–3 (AMP)

CHAPTER 9

In Closing

He shall not break his word.
– Numbers 30:2

VOW, noun

1. A solemn promise made to God or to some deity; an act by which one consecrates or devotes himself, absolutely or conditionally, wholly or in part, for a longer or shorter time, to some act, service, or condition

– Webster's Dictionary 1913[1]

It is vital to the success of your marriage that you believe you must be committed for the long term. Commit yourself to walking this process out. Do everything you can do to receive all God's blessings for your marriage. I believe that if you apply God's Word to every part of your own growth and that of your marriage, there is no way you are going to feel as if leaving your marriage is in your best interest. What is in your best interest is to believe that those God has brought together stay together.

Make having a great marriage your priority. Settle within yourself that you have made the right choice and that you have made a commitment you will never break. Decide that you want to be engaged in your relationship. Treat every day as a new opportunity to make your marriage work. Be committed to doing the things you do not feel like doing. There is never a time to give up on your relationship. Connect your godly desires for your marriage to the greater vision, and let your faith carry you through its realization. Understand that everything may not go your way, but settle from within that it is going to be okay. With all God's resources at hand, you have everything you need to develop and grow your relationship.

- Train your mind up in the way it should go, and eventually you will see the first fruits of your efforts.
- Do not waste another second wondering if the relationship that you have before you won't work out.
- Take pride in feeling alive, and attract the thing that you desire by being a godly, loving spouse.
- Trust in the will of God and take ownership for your actions.
- Pride yourself in loving your spouse and understand the mission of your marriage.
- Celebrate the small victories along the journey.
- Take the initiative in making good changes.

- Remove any habit or obstacle that prevents you from being great.
- Stay humble.
- Stay full of hope and faith.
- Put forth the effort into bringing your vision to reality.

I would like to leave you with this verse:

If a man vows a vow to the Lord or swears an oath to bind himself by a pledge, he shall not break his word. He shall do according to all that proceeds out of his mouth.

— – NUMBERS 30:2 (ESV)

This Scripture reveals the severity of not honoring or fulfilling the words that you have spoken. When you said I do, you summited a vow not only unto your spouse but unto the Lord. Be a responsible spouse and take your marriage seriously. Be unwilling to compromise for the sake of others' opinions. I assure you that if you keep the faith and hold up your end of the agreement, God, who is not like man, will do His part to ensure your marriage is a success.

God bless and keep the faith.

Dennis S. Nickens

BEING COMMITTED TO ONE ANOTHER

Lifelong commitment is not what most people think it is.

It's not waking up every morning to make breakfast and eat together.

It's not cuddling in bed until both of you fall asleep.

It's not a clean home filled with laughter and lovemaking every day.

It's someone who steals all the covers and snores.

It's slammed doors and a few harsh words at times.

It's stubbornly disagreeing and giving each other the silent treatment until your hearts heal and then offering forgiveness.

It's coming home to the same person every day who you know loves and cares about you, in spite of and because of who you are.

It's laughing about the one time you accidentally did something stupid.

It's about dirty laundry and unmade beds.

It's about helping each other with the hard work of life.

It's about swallowing the nagging words instead of saying something out loud.

It's about eating the easiest meal you can make and sitting down together at a late hour because you both had a crazy day.

It's about having an emotional breakdown, and your love lies down with you, holds you, and tells you everything is going to be okay, and you believe them.

It's about still loving someone even though sometimes they make you feel absolutely insane.

Loving someone ... it's not always easy; sometimes it's hard. But it is amazing, comforting, and one of the best things you will ever experience.

Acknowledgments

Foremost, I would like to thank my Lord and Savior, Jesus Christ. Without the spirit of God in my life, I would be a ship without a sail. You are the reason for the season and the purpose of my existence.

I would like to express my sincere gratitude to my immediate family. My parents taught me at a young age that it takes a village to raise a child. I am thankful for the village that helped develop me. You were patient with me when I strayed off the right path, and you moti- vated me to be the best version of myself that I could be. You supported me as I weathered the storms of life.

To friends, mentors, pastors, military leaders, teach- ers, and the people who told me that I did not have the ability to make it, your words were the fuel I needed to be able to look in the mirror and be honest with myself. Our paths crossing was not a mistake; it was for a divine purpose, and I would not change anything, because I am doing what I was created to do because of it.

To my blended family, what a privilege it is to be able to have a relationship with you. You accepted me for who I am, and what a joy it is for us to dwell together in unity. I trust with all my heart that we will do our parts in remaining connected to the right source, who moti- vates us to do things that gratify.

To my boys, I pray you understand that my goal is to train you up in the way you should go in order to ensure that you have a firm foundation that can sustain you. I view you as a gift from God, and it is my responsibility to ensure that you contain the endurance to run after your dreams with the mindset that you are preparing to be great. Dwell in your greatness and change the world for the better.

To my spouse, Barbara Nickens, the queen bee of the house, you are truly the MVP of our marriage. You have a heart of gold, and you are the incubator of life—you give birth to things that make my life better. You are a precious flower, and I thank God for you, understanding that I obtain favor from God because of you. I pray that you feel that I love you the way the Bible instructs me to love you—"as Christ loved the church and gave himself up for her" (Ephesians 5:25).

About the Author

Dennis S. Nickens, MBA, is the CEO of Total Package LLC, a clothing company. He is also a program analyst with the federal government, a service member, and the author of two books: Doing It God's Way, It Works: Friendship transitioning into a healthy marriageand Unbroken Vows: Keeping it together.

Dennis's parents played an active role in his develop- ment growing up, modeling commitment to God above all. He saw how it affected not only their marriage, but also everyone they came in contact with, for the better. From this experience, he learned that anything that's worth having is going to require persistence and com- mitment.

It is Dennis's purpose in life to run the race he has been called to run—to encourage couples and assist them in believing that they have a right to the Tree of Life, along with the authority to demand and expect that God's promises will come to pass and work out in their favor. A devoted husband and a believer in the Most High, Dennis believes that every relationship has the opportunity to be something amazing, but that both participants are required to put forth the effort to make it happen.

Dennis's motto in life is: "It's not about me, it's all about Him." Jesus is the one who died for him, so He is the one his life should be about. He knows that the more he understands who He is, the better off his relationships will be. The same goes for you.

Follow
    Email: Dennis@tp-ll.com

Can You Help?
Reviews are everything to an author because they mean a book is given more visibility. If you enjoyed this book, please review it on your favorite book review sites and tell your friends about it. Thank you!

Notes

1. MARRIAGE IS...

1. [1]American Dictionary of the English Language, Webster's Dictionary 1828 Online edition, s.v. "marriage," http://webstersdiction- ary1828.com/Dictionary/marriage.

2. LOVE IS...

1. American Dictionary of the English Language, Webster's Dictionary 1828 Online edition, s.v. "love," http://webstersdiction- ary1828.com/Dictionary/love.
2. [3] Joseph M. Scriven, "What a Friend We Have in Jesus," 1855.

3. PURITY

1. American Dictionary of the English Language, Webster's Dictionary 1828 Online edition, s.v. "purity," http://webstersdiction- ary1828.com/Dictionary/purity.
2. Dr. Shirley Glass, "Afterword: Mini-Guide to Safe Friendships and a Secure Marriage," ShirleyGlass.com, accessed October 25, 2019, http://shirleyglass.com/afterword.htm.

4. COMMUNICATION

1. American Dictionary of the English Language,Webster's Dictionary 1913 Online edition, s.v. "communicate," http:// https://www.web- sters1913.com/words/Communicate.
2. [7] Webster's 1913, s.v. "Friend," accessed October 30, 2019, https://www.websters1913.com/words/Friend.

5. JESUS, THE BRIDEGROOM

1. American Dictionary of the English Language,Webster's Dictionary 1913 Online edition, s.v. "groom," http:// https://www.web- sters1913.com/words/Groom.

6. YOUR SHARED VISION

1. American Dictionary of the English Language,Webster's Dictionary 1913 Online edition, s.v. "vision," http:// https://www.web- sters1913.com/words/Vision.

7. FIGHT FOR YOUR MARRIAGE

1. American Dictionary of the English Language,Webster's Dictionary 1913 Online edition, s.v. "fight," https://www.web- sters1913.com/words/Fight.

8. DON'T QUIT!

1. American Dictionary of the English Language,Webster's Dictionary 1913 Online edition, s.v. "quit," http:// https://www.web- sters1913.com/words/Quit.

9. IN CLOSING

1. American Dictionary of the English Language,Webster's Dictionary 1913 Online edition, s.v. "vow," http:// https://www.web- sters1913.com/words/Vow.